Language Awareness

All too often, schools make decisions about language without a proper understanding of the issues involved. *Language Awareness at School* addresses this problem by exploring a range of topics related to language, helping teachers to make informed choices about how to best support their students in becoming more confident, aware speakers and writers.

Written in collaboration by an academic linguist and an experienced teacher, this essential book combines professional experience and academic expertise to demonstrate how a language-aware approach to education has the potential to transform both whole-school policy and classroom practice.

Chapters explore such questions as the misconceptions surrounding the use of 'Standard English', teachers' and students' local accents, the development of cross-curricular speaking and writing skills and how to reinvigorate Modern Foreign Languages. This book also works to undo damaging prejudices about how students speak, instead highlighting opportunities to encourage students to notice, examine and debate language issues.

Language Awareness at School is a crucial read for all teachers, trainee teachers and school leadership teams who want to make more informed decisions regarding language issues in schools.

Tim Marr is Visiting Professor in Applied Linguistics at Universidad Icesi, Cali, Colombia. He was formerly director of the MA TESOL programme at London Metropolitan University and has over 30 years' experience in teaching and researching language and linguistics, as well as training language teachers. He has co-authored several books on linguistics and TESOL.

Steve Collins is Head of English at Bishop Luffa School, Chichester, where he teaches Key Stages 3 to 5, specialising in A Level English Language. He has taught in secondary schools for 20 years, and also taught EFL in Peru and the UK. He contributed a chapter on sentence-level analysis to the Routledge book *Teaching English Language and Literature 16–19*.

'It's refreshing to read such a coherent and informed vision of what language teaching can and should look like in our schools — be it in English classrooms, foreign language lessons or across the whole curriculum. Not a gap or a deficit in sight! Instead, Marr and Collins offer and exemplify a compelling argument for the kind of language-informed practice that will benefit students everywhere.

I'd recommend this book to all teachers looking to raise their own language awareness. School leaders, in particular, will find it an invaluable resource to help them navigate a path that moves schools beyond misleading and damaging gap and deficit narratives.'

Andrew McCallum
Director of the English and Media Centre, London

'Drawing on a range of historical and recent research and using a number of topical and well-presented examples, Marr and Collins examine debates about the use of Standard English, zero-tolerance approaches to language use through word bans, misconceptions such as 'correct English', the place of linguistics in the English curriculum, and the value of learning languages other than English. The book offers a very useful reference point for teachers interested in developing their own linguistic knowledge in order to make their classrooms more inclusive, and for middle and senior leaders looking to raise language awareness at whole-school level.'

Marcello Giovanelli
Reader in Literary Linguistics, Aston University, UK

'A precise balance of linguistic principles and practical direction, this highly readable work convincingly shows that literacy must go hand-in-hand with language awareness. A strong command of these skills forms the gateway to social mobility, and our young people deserve nothing less. If only this inspiring book had been available at the start of my career, it would have saved me years of experimentation.'

Mark Arnull
Headteacher, Q3 Academy Great Barr, West Midlands, UK

Language Awareness at School

A Practical Guide for Teachers and School Leaders

Tim Marr and Steve Collins

Routledge
Taylor & Francis Group

LONDON AND NEW YORK

Designed cover image: © Getty Images

First published 2023
by Routledge
4 Park Square, Milton Park, Abingdon, Oxon OX14 4RN

and by Routledge
605 Third Avenue, New York, NY 10158

Routledge is an imprint of the Taylor & Francis Group, an informa business

British Library Cataloguing-in-Publication Data
A catalogue record for this book is available from the British Library

Library of Congress Cataloging-in-Publication Data
Names: Marr, Tim, author. | Collins, Steven, 1960- author.
Title: Language awareness at school : a practical guide for teachers and school leaders / Tim Marr, Steve Collins.
Description: New York : Routledge, 2024. | Includes bibliographical references and index.
Identifiers: LCCN 2022051098 (print) | LCCN 2022051099 (ebook) | ISBN 9781032062327 (Hardback) | ISBN 9781032062334 (Paperback) | ISBN 9781003201281 (eBook)
Subjects: LCSH: Language arts--United States. | Language awareness--United States. | Linguistics--Study and teaching--United States. | Language and education.
Classification: LCC LB1576 .M3782 2024 (print) | LCC LB1576 (ebook) | DDC 372.6--dc23/eng/20230120
LC record available at https://lccn.loc.gov/2022051098
LC ebook record available at https://lccn.loc.gov/2022051099

ISBN: 978-1-032-06232-7 (hbk)
ISBN: 978-1-032-06233-4 (pbk)
ISBN: 978-1-003-20128-1 (ebk)

DOI: 10.4324/9781003201281

Typeset in Melior
by SPi Technologies India Pvt Ltd (Straive)

Printed in the United Kingdom
by Henry Ling Limited

Contents

Acknowledgements

We are hugely grateful to Fiona English for her help and support at various points, and especially for reading and commenting on the finished manuscript. Thanks are also due to David Oakey and Ben Coulthard (thanks again, Ben!) for helpful contributions, and to the teachers who were kind enough to answer our questions and comment on earlier drafts, especially Mark Arnull, Chloë Barnett, Jen Sherlock and Jas Stone.

We are grateful to the anonymous reviewers whose comments on our original proposal helped guide us in some very important ways. There are also others who helped form our ideas without necessarily being aware of it, among them Lennie Butler, Holofernes, Jorge Dragão, Timothy Taylor and Brian and Sylvia Martin.

Thanks to our editors at Routledge, Annamarie Kino and Lauren Redhead, for their cheerful encouragement. And thanks from Tim to Ana and from Steve to Melanie, George, Finn and Joe for your love and patience!

Introduction: Why we're talking about language

1.1 Students' language at school: a letter and a notice

What do you think might be your initial reaction if, as a parent, you were to receive this letter (Box 1.1) from the head teacher of a school?

Box 1.1 A letter

If you hear your children saying the following phrases or words in the left-hand column please correct them using the phrase or word in the right-hand column. I'm sure if we tackle this problem together we will make progress.

Incorrect	Correct
I **done** that	This should be, I **have done** that or I **did** that
I **seen** that	This should be, I **have seen** that or I **saw** that
Yous	The word you is NEVER plural, e.g. we should say, '**You** lot come here!'
Dropping the 'th'	'School finishes at **free** fifteen' should be 'School finishes at **three** fifteen'
Gizit ere	Please **give** me **it**
I **dunno**	This should be, I **don't know**
Letta, butta	**Letter, butter** etc
Your	Your late should be, **you're** late
Werk, shert etc	I will wear my **shirt** for **work**

And how might you react if you saw this notice (Box 1.2) on display in a school?

DOI: 10.4324/9781003201281-1

> **Box 1.2 A notice**
>
> *Positively no chirpsing or jamming on the stairwells, do not wear the creps from your drum in these ends; extra behaviour in the corridor will not be allowed.*

Would you be amused? Delighted? Outraged? Intrigued? How you respond to these messages probably depends on how you feel about things like 'correctness' in language, or the way groups of young people speak these days, or discipline in schools. But let's consider the intentions behind them. What might these two communications, in their different ways, be attempting to do?

Clearly, both of the texts are designed to make us think about use of language – one very explicitly, the other implicitly. But which is most likely to be effective? Actually, given the focus of this book, perhaps we should be asking a different question. Perhaps it should be: which is most likely to lead to increased awareness of language? We'll discuss exactly what we mean by 'language awareness' in more detail in a moment (in Section 1.5.4 below), but for now let's take it to mean something like sensitivity to language and the way language works. So in this case, we mean noticing things about language and appropriacy, thinking about how we adjust our language to the various contexts we find ourselves operating in, considering how we select from our communicative resources in order to achieve a particular effect or outcome.

We would suggest that the two communications function in very different ways. The most immediately noticeable thing about the first one is how confused it is about language. The letter writer states that the subject is children's *speech* ('if you hear your child saying…'), but some of the features highlighted for correction are errors of *writing* ('letta, butta'; 'werk, shert'; 'your late'). And some of the recommendations are strangely misplaced or poorly described. The 'th' in 'three' is not 'dropped', as the writer says, but replaced by the sound /f/ – a common speech feature in English known to linguists as 'th-fronting'. The word 'you' can obviously be a plural ('You have all done very well!') – what they mean is that it is never pluralised with an -s (in Standard English at least). The issue of 'please give me it' for 'gizit ere' or 'I did that' for 'I done that' is a simple one of standard English grammar versus local dialect – that is, an issue of using a linguistic register that is appropriate to the context. But the head teacher never mentions this crucial aspect of the question, and makes no reference to appropriacy at all, opting instead for a straightforward request that children be 'corrected' for everyday dialectal usage, even at home.

So this letter is hardly the work of someone who is themself sensitive to language and the way language works. There's something even more striking about it, though, which is the underlying attitude to language that it suggests. It does not set out to start a conversation about the children's use of language, nor to help children (and parents) move towards a mature understanding of how language is adapted to social context. Rather, it attempts expressly to prohibit and exclude certain forms of language from school life – and even from the home, as we have just noted – as if they were self-evidently undesirable and sub-standard, not to be entertained under any circumstances.

There is *concern* for language here, certainly, but there is very little obvious *interest* in language.

The second is a very different kind of affair. It is deliberately much less obvious in its purpose, but you might argue that what really distinguishes it from the head teacher's letter is that it is intended to provoke debate and reflection. It's funny, of course – we, and the students and even teachers it is aimed at, are not used to seeing black London 'street talk' in the formal context of a behaviour-regulating school notice – but it also has the serious intention of making us think about language. Specifically, it makes us think about why, exactly, we're not used to encountering these particular words in this particular context. To put it in linguistic terms, it invites us to think about register, context and appropriacy. And unlike the letter sent home, it shows genuine interest in language and how it is used.

1.1.1 About the letter and the notice

Now, one of our language-related communications is genuine and actually exists, or existed. It was written to parents by the head of a school in Middlesbrough, and you can find it online.[1] There is something of a history here, and you might well have come across other announcements of this type over the last few years – they tend to make a bit of a stir on social media and in the press, even if only briefly. There was the Harris Academy sign (Figure 1.1), which you might remember from the extraordinary fuss it caused when it was put up outside a school in south London. Tim wrote about it then, in a book called *Why Do Linguistics?*[2] and lots of other linguists have also had hours of fun analysing it.

And you can see why it caused a fuss – 'Banned Words' is an attention-grabbing, combative phrase, indicative of a hostile approach to the language the school's students habitually use. It doesn't invite or encourage reflection or debate (though it may attract resentment and derision). It certainly *could* lead to a fruitful discussion about language – but equally certainly, that is not its intention. The Ark All Saints Academy in south London, meanwhile, not content with outlawing classroom use of distinctively Caribbean phrases like 'Oh my days' and 'He cut his eyes at me',

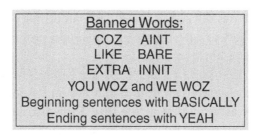

Figure 1.1 Sign outside a school in south London.

went the whole hog and forbade students from starting sentences with natural fillers such as 'Ermmm…' or 'You see…', for all the world as if speaking were just the same as writing.[3] British TV viewers are, of course, well used to hearing political correspondent Robert Peston using all manner of such fillers, but still speaking with coherence, authority and some style. But again, the school's intention was not to create a conversation about how different people use language.

So there's quite a history of real, genuine attempts to control pupils' language use without giving space for further discussion. Our example in Box 1.2, though, is made up – which is a pity! It was suggested to us by a former teacher at the very school in south London where the 'Banned Words' sign actually appeared (and which, as you might have been able to work out, has a high proportion of African-Caribbean pupils). This teacher, unhappy with the disparaging approach to students' language that the 'Banned Words' sign represented, considered the possibilities of what a genuinely enlightening school language policy could be like. He subsequently came up with the idea of the 'no chirpsing or jamming' notice as a light-hearted (but in the end, quite serious) way to engage students in debate and discussion about language use. Seeing their own characteristic slang and colloquial terms in the unfamiliar context of an official notice, he reasoned (*creps* are training shoes, your *drum* is your home, *chirpsing* is flirting), would catch the attention of the students – and perhaps even the teachers – and encourage them to think about language and social context.

1.2 Language attitudes and the school

Why have we started a book about language awareness at school with these examples? Well, the difference between the imagined notice and the two genuine communications encapsulates some fundamental questions at the heart of thinking and policy making about language and the school. Is the students' language – and that of the teachers, for that matter – to be treated as a problem, or as a pedagogic resource? Do we welcome the language (and languages) of the community into the community of the school, or do we fight tooth and nail to keep them out? Is the policy designed to control and police students' use of language, or to encourage them to reflect on and learn about it?

Consider this Twitter exchange from 2021. It started with a complaint about schoolchildren's speech, in particular 'that whole "yes bruv innit". Street talk'. The complainant went on: 'Give me a break. I was in primary school in the 80s. We had it drilled into us how to write, spell, grammar and pronunciation'. A sociolinguist noticed the tweet and responded:

Hi! Linguist here. Language variation is natural and systematic. People use language to convey aspects of their identity. Kids also know how to 'style-shift' without explicit instruction. So whilst they may use 'bruv' with their mates, they're unlikely to in a job interview.

Perfectly normal youth speech (in this case, the variety known to sociolinguists as Multicultural London English or MLE) is routinely criticised in this way, and regarded with suspicion or even disdain ('Give me a break'). We're not actually entirely convinced that the linguist's comments tell the whole story (and so we'll return to this exchange in Chapter 4), but his response does make an essential point – that language variation is natural and, most importantly, systematic. It's not chaotic; it's not that there are no rules. If anything, style-shifting (analogous to code-switching, which we refer to below) suggests that young people understand the rules and are playing with them.

As the Twitter linguist also points out, changing speech styles can also of course be seen as an act of identity, or the performance of identity, to use terms from the field of sociolinguistics. Speakers express themselves, and signal their relationship to other speakers and groups of speakers, through their choice of language in any given context. We do, you do, *everyone* does. It's just that more socially elevated groups of people don't tend to have their way of speaking attacked with angry contempt. Here's an extract from an article about public school slang, published online by a private prep school consultancy, that sounds amused, indulgent, even admiring of this exotic youth sociolect.[4] The article begins by noting that 'Since they first opened their doors, public schools across the land have been adding to the Queen's English with bizarre expressions of their own', and goes on to explain rather neatly the role of a sociolect in creating and maintaining a sense of group identity:

> A sense of belonging is vital at these institutions – and what could be more bonding than a universal lingo that is adopted by all pupils, exists only within the school's hallowed walls and is largely incomprehensible to outsiders?

Well, quite. And we are then treated to examples of 'some of the strangest school slang around', from a fairly limited set of these exclusive establishments:

> **Banco** – *used at*: Charterhouse *meaning*: homework
> **Beak** – *used at*: Eton College, Charterhouse, Harrow School *meaning*: teacher
> **Bims** – *used at*: Wellington College *meaning*: weekly inter-house sports fixtures
> **Chambers** – *used at*: Eton College *meaning*: mid-morning break
> **College Pig** – *used at*: Wellington College *meaning*: school prefect

And so on – you get the idea.

Shouldn't schools be asking their students to reflect on their language choices, to think and talk about how language is used, to develop a deeper understanding of how language is appropriate to context? Apart from anything else, 'being shown that your language is interesting and skilful builds confidence and self-esteem', as the sociolinguistics professor Emma Moore (who tweets as @SociolingEm) put it in a tweet on teaching grammar at school. And yet, a good many schools don't do this kind of inclusive, critical language work – even though it is, of course, a core

A level English Language topic – preferring instead to ignore their students' language or attempt to police it or restrain it. And in this they have been encouraged by politicians and even successive ministers for education.

1.3 Language awareness, and the lack of it

Why might this be? Well, we should make it quite clear at this point that we're not having a go at these schools, or at schools in general. Rather, the lack of language awareness in some schools simply reflects a generalised lack of language awareness throughout society. The problem we want to address in this book, though, is that this lack of understanding causes difficulty when language issues come up at school, which they do, all the time, every day – and this is a book about language and the school.

Schools are, by the very nature of things, visible: embedded in communities, they are under constant observation and appraisal, so even a minor error can end up being exposed to public scrutiny. Back in 2018 the press reported gleefully how a hapless academy school teacher produced a literacy homework exercise in the form of a crossword which turned out to be only semi-literate itself, producing answers like 'In contrast they had are prone to earthquakes, they do not have tremor-proof houses' and 'People were not prepared well enough for the disaster, on the contrary they did not deserve it'. For good measure, the instructions asked pupils to 'Complete the crossword by interesting one of the words below into the sentences'. When parents complained, the head teacher managed to dig an even deeper hole. The *Daily Telegraph* reported:

> Last night, Mr Williams told the Telegraph: "The academy accepts that the homework provided did include some errors. Whilst this is an unfortunate and regrettable incident, it has been appropriately addressed and the school shall continue to support learning at home."[5]

The teacher's original mistake plays into an established media narrative about declining standards of literacy, but of course the response is entertaining, too. The semi-apology is couched in tone-deaf corporate-speak, and the deliciously misjudged 'shall' instead of 'will' in the head teacher's riposte (presumably he thinks it sounds formal and decisive, rather than pompously inappropriate) is the icing on the cake. But we're not just talking about a poor grasp of English grammar or the English language here, we're talking about a poor grasp of the whole field of language itself – and sometimes, as we shall see, this lack of language awareness is serious, and has consequences.

We started with the issue of rules governing students' speech because that's something of a hot topic at the moment, given the government-inspired push to mandate Standard English in classrooms, but in this book we want to go well beyond that one particular aspect of language in schools. In illustrating some of the areas where a general lack of understanding about language is often evident, we hope to show how a language awareness approach can lead to staff making better and more informed decisions, and in turn to students being better and more confident speakers and writers.

Here are a few of the language-related snippets and incidents that we have come across at various times, the kind of thing that got us thinking about how language issues are perceived, taught and dealt with in the public sphere. Some of them are directly school-related, some are not. We'll make a few comments on each, then link them to the detailed further discussion in the book proper.

1.3.1 Speaking and writing

- The website babycenter.com advises parents that by a certain age, 'Your child should use varied, complete sentences' and 'use correct grammar most of the time'.

This online advice manages to be so wildly imprecise that it is likely to do nothing but increase or even *create* parental worry and anxiety. Who on earth normally goes around speaking in 'complete sentences'? (Writing is another matter, of course.) In 2018 the then Education Secretary was almost as imprecise and misleading when he declared that 'it is a persistent scandal that we have children starting school not able to communicate in full sentences'. And what exactly do the people at babycenter.com mean by 'correct grammar'? Do they mean Standard English? Or do they mean grammar that conforms with the local dialect, whatever that might be? When speaking is confused with writing, and 'correct' language with standard language, children are apt to end up being disadvantaged for speaking normally, or for the mere fact of using local dialect. We dig into this whole matter in Chapter 2, and try to establish some frameworks to help develop more precise, linguistically informed thinking on this topic.

And this leads us on to...

1.3.2 A 'zero tolerance' policy

- The *Guardian* reported on the case of a head teacher from a school in the Black Country (in the English Midlands), who banned the local dialect from his classrooms on the grounds that this would help raise literacy standards. The head was quoted as saying: 'We'd been looking at our literacy standards and we wanted to talk to parents about some of the confusion that happens when children are talking to their mates in the playground'. Again, notice how speaking and writing get muddled up and treated as being fundamentally the same kind of thing, subject to the same rules and conventions. 'When it comes to phonics and English lessons it can be very confusing for the children. When they are reading phonics, it's incorrect, so we think it's better for them this way. We're not stopping them talking to their friends in the playground how they want to'. The last certainly comes as a relief. The head teacher finishes, though, with an ominous: 'We're just saying that in the classroom we'll correct them.'[6]

The context of this report, as with some of the examples we looked at earlier, was a letter sent to parents from another Midlands school which announced a 'Zero tolerance' approach to local dialect use in the classroom (Figure 1.2 - we've deleted the name of the school).[7]

Actually, despite the stern-looking (and scary-sounding) 'Zero tolerance' slogan – and the confusion between regional dialect and slang, and between spoken and written norms – the letter does in fact display a measure of sensitivity towards the idea of language and context. It explicitly acknowledges that '[w]e value the local dialect but are encouraging the children to learn the skill of turning it on and off in different situations' and emphasises 'using the right language for the right context'.

What we are doing at

- Recently we have asked each class teacher to write a list of the top ten most damaging phrases used by children in their class:

1. "they was" instead of "they were"
2. "I cor do that" instead of "I cant do that"
3. "Ya" instead of "you"
4. "gonna" instead of "going to"
5. "woz" instead of "was"
6. "I day" instead of "I didn't"
7. "I ain't" instead of "I haven't"
8. "somefink" instead of "something"
9. "It wor me" instead of "it wasn't me"
10. "ay?" instead of "pardon?"

We want children in our school to have the best start possible: understanding when it is and is not acceptable to use slang or colloquial language. We value the local dialect but are encouraging children to learn the skill of turning it on and off in different situations. —Using the right language for the right context– Formal English in the classroom and slang in the school playground.

We are introducing a 'Zero tolerance' policy in the classroom to get children out of the habit of using phrases like the ones listed above. Your support with this is invaluable in helping your child go into the world equipped with the appropriate use of language so that they are not disadvantaged.

Never Settle For Less Than Your Best

Figure 1.2 Letter sent home by school.

That is, the school presumably wants the children to develop the facility that linguists would call 'code-switching' or 'style-shifting'. So you can see where they are going with this, but it's a heavy-handed approach, to say the very least. 'We are introducing a zero tolerance policy in the classroom to get children out of the habit of using phrases like the ones listed above' displays a pretty unforgiving, not to say punitive attitude towards local speech norms.

In the newspaper interview with the Black Country head teacher, though, what really leaps out is the phrase: 'it can be very confusing for the children'. All right, they get confused – so why would you not take this opportunity to educate them? Why not educate them about register and appropriacy to context, about how standard language differs from slang, and from regional usage? Why not educate them about accents and dialects? Why not educate them about *language*? It is a bizarre decision in both linguistic and educational terms to simply banish certain words from the classroom. Rather, students' use of slang and dialect terms should be regarded as a learning opportunity – the starting point of what could be a hugely profitable discussion about how language is used, perceived, and judged in social terms by the wider community. Beginning in Chapter 2, and continuing into Chapter 3, we explore the linguistic principles that underlie this way of thinking about language use and language education.

1.3.3 A child prodigy?

• In 2019 the Indian newspaper *The Asian Age* reported on a child language learning prodigy. The 'eight-year-old polyglot' from Chennai in India, Niall Thoguluva, explained that he used YouTube to help him learn a 'plethora' of languages. He said: 'I do not know how my interest in languages began. I can read and write over 106 languages and can fluently speak 10 languages. I am currently learning five new languages.'[8]

Does anyone really believe that someone – let alone an eight-year-old – can 'read and write over 106 languages' and 'fluently speak' ten? What does 'read and write' actually mean in this case, and how are we defining 'fluently' here? Now, of course, we can pick holes in one naïve and uncritical newspaper report, but it is actually indicative of a much broader phenomenon. People often tend to overestimate *vastly* what a child can learn in modern foreign language (MFL) classes – and particularly in primary MFL classes, compulsory at KS2 in England since 2014 – because they have been led to believe that children 'learn languages effortlessly' or 'soak up languages like a sponge'. In fact, generalised ignorance about how language learning works and what it entails can have serious consequences. In school contexts, specifically, it can lead to bad decisions being made – things like starting too soon, supporting teachers too little, expecting too much, and relying on the magic of supposed 'immersion' to achieve effortless acquisition of new grammar and vocabulary. And an early, bad experience of language learning can put young people off languages for life. In Chapter 7 we try to strengthen the case for rational and effective approaches to foreign language teaching by exploring some of the myths and the hard truths around early language learning.

And it is not just about when you start learning another language; it's also about which language you choose.

1.3.4 Choosing a language

• According to Sir Martin Sorrell, businessman and founder of WPP plc, the world's largest advertising and PR group: 'Chinese and computer code are the only two languages the next generation should need.'

Sir Martin's assertion is an eye-popping one in more than one way, of course, but let's focus on the claim about Chinese. As we will show, people routinely make grand claims for Chinese which have little basis in reality: and anyone who thinks a few hours' Chinese teaching each week is going to have radical implications for children's future prosperity is heading for disappointment. But there's a wider problem here. Schools and pupils quite often make poor decisions about which foreign language(s) to teach or learn, because they don't have sufficient sociolinguistic awareness to help them think about the way languages are used internationally and the value and benefits that come with learning particular languages. In Chapters 6 and 7 we address the whole question of why exactly MFLs are so important, and how to go about selecting the one or ones which best suit a particular school or pupil. In particular, we will suggest that a clearer understanding of the sociolinguistic background, communicated clearly to pupils and their parents, might help arrest the decline in take-up of languages at GCSE and A level.

1.3.5 What do English teachers teach?

• In a newspaper article about the teaching of Spelling, Pronunciation and Grammar (or SPaG for short), an author explains: 'I wasn't taught grammar at school and this never prevented me from expressing myself and earning my living as a writer'. Meanwhile an English teacher tells us, only semi-jokingly, 'I don't do terminology'.

Even some English teachers are reluctant to teach English language, and specifically grammar, because they think of themselves as specialists in literature, or creative writing, or self-expression in general. Some of them, the research suggests, are even hazy about what 'grammar' actually is. And how do we form a bridge between the 'language' aspects of English and the rest? We consider the whole question of what 'English' denotes in Chapter 5, dig into a bit of the history of the subject, and try to lay out a framework. Specifically, we argue that a language awareness approach to English teaching might help lend coherence and cohesiveness to what can sometimes appear to be a rather fractured subject.

1.3.6 Teachers are obliged to model 'competent' and 'articulate' speech – but who decides what that is?

- As reported by the *Independent*: 'A teacher has been told to tone down her northern accent as a result of criticism by school inspectors. The teacher, who is working in west Berkshire but hails from Cumbria, has been set this by her school as one of her "targets" to improve performance, her union said today.'[9] And a teacher told us, the authors: 'A Level Literature students have been known to mock the accents of their teachers at my school. For instance, a former colleague was visibly upset when students mimicked her accent, even though she was the only faculty member with a PhD in English Literature.'

Students do indeed sometimes mock their teachers' speech, but sometimes the hostility to a teacher's accent or variety of English can come from inspectors, management or a senior mentor. Indeed, over the years, there has been a good deal of media reporting on prejudice and discrimination towards the accents of largely working-class teachers across the UK. The DfE's Teachers' Standards document states that teachers should model 'articulate' speech – but who decides what is articulate, and on what grounds? In Chapter 2, we argue that situations like these ones are best addressed not by disciplinary measures against pupils or performance targets for staff, but by open, language-aware and sociolinguistically informed discussion, in the classroom and in the school as a whole.

And by the same token...

1.3.7 Home languages at school

- A senior lecturer in languages in education at Goldsmiths, University of London, says: 'The UK's failure to value the 300 languages (approximately) spoken in the country is leading to an erosion of language skills over generations, to the detriment of individual speakers and society as a whole.' In order to tackle this problem, 'there could be potential for supplementary schools – believed to number over 3,000 in the UK – and mainstream schools to work together, to allow the latter to broaden the range of their language offer and encourage the valuing of literacy in all languages'.[10]

Schools do sometimes introduce heritage language classes, either alone or with the help of local community helpers, in order to connect with their minority language pupils and be seen to validate their home language and culture. However, too often interest in the classes dwindles and children opt for English monolingualism.

Everyone ends up disappointed – children, parents, the school and the community helpers. What is going wrong? Some structured insight from sociolinguistics into differential language prestige and the question of language hierarchies could help explain a lot, as could an understanding of what 'standard' languages actually are, how they come into being, and how they differ from dialects. The political-ideological aspect of language is lurking in the background, and everyone therefore needs to approach this with care, respect and a measure of political sensitivity (but not naivety). In Chapter 7 we try to offer some background context and constructive advice.

1.3.8 What is 'academic' English?

• Figure 1.3 shows a sample from a popular series of guides to academic writing.

But is a 'right' and 'wrong' approach like this really the best way to go about teaching children how to write in an academic style? Is 'kings and queens' always wrong in a history essay, while 'monarchs' is always right? And are phrasal verbs really always to be avoided? As we illustrate in Chapter 4, teaching children about 'academic English' cries out for a language-aware approach, for teaching about e.g. register, style and disciplinary discourses, rather than a mechanical checklist of do's and don'ts.

In fact, we will be arguing in this book for a language awareness approach to *all* these issues, using the insights that linguistics can provide. And in Chapter 8 we will suggest ways in which it can be implemented across the school. But how did we get to this point? That is to say, why are linguistics perspectives not routinely incorporated into most schools' approaches to these and other language issues and language problems?

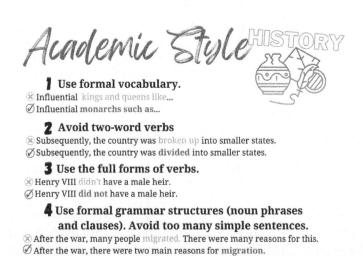

Figure 1.3 Academic style sheet. Adapted from The EAP Foundation.

1.4 Getting to this point: the linguist and the layperson

In her book *Verbal Hygiene* the linguist Professor Deborah Cameron recounts how she once on an impulse dropped into an exhibition in London's Conway Hall entitled 'The Use and Abuse of Language'. Once inside she was approached by one of the language enthusiasts and 'concerned citizens' who had helped put on the exhibition. Upon learning what she did for a living, the man exclaimed: 'A linguist! How marvellous! Do tell me what linguists are doing to combat the abuse of language.' She goes on: 'Embarrassed, I made my excuses and left'. This little anecdote encapsulates very neatly the way academic linguists and the public often find themselves talking at cross-purposes, which is precisely why Cameron included it in her book. So what was going on here? Let's try and unpack it a little.

It's a fair bet that the organisation that mounted the exhibition was the Queen's English Society, or another one very much like it. The Society states on its website that part of its purpose is to 'educate the public in... correct and elegant usage', 'to encourage the speaking and writing of English characterised by grammatical correctness and proper usage of words and expressions', and that it 'strongly advocates... the need for all teachers of all subjects to correct students' English'. The man at the exhibition, upon learning that Cameron was a linguist – that is, a professional academic specialising in the study of language, as we discuss at 1.5.2 below – assumed that he had found a natural ally, and that academic linguists would, of course, share the same goals as the Society.

So why would the professor of linguistics make her excuses and leave? Well, here's the problem. Linguists as a breed strive to be descriptive about language, not prescriptive. In other words, they're primarily interested in what people actually say, not what is or isn't considered 'correct and elegant'. So they'd be very reluctant to give you advice about how you should say things, just as they wouldn't want to be drawn on old chestnuts like which language is the most logical or the most expressive. They wouldn't think that there is a 'best' variety of English, any more than astronomers think that there is a best asteroid, or chemists that there is a best element. And they *certainly* wouldn't think that some people's ways of speaking are sloppy, lazy or just plain wrong, and therefore need to be 'corrected'.

In short, linguistics is one of those academic disciplines where a good deal of what is believed by ordinary people to be obvious is regarded by the professionals as being misguided or mistaken. And, of course, vice versa: a fair amount of what academic linguists hold as self-evident is regarded by many laypeople, and particularly people like the Queen's English Society, as preposterous. As Cameron points out in her book, people really do care about language, which is surely a good thing in itself – but they tend to care more about what she calls the 'right and wrong, good and bad' part of it than anything else. So, for example, they often don't like the way non-standard language is used, whereas linguists tend to be endlessly fascinated and excited by it. Linguistics sometimes seems to be impenetrable, and linguists to be deliberately contrary, or stuck in their ivory towers.

'Linguists lament slang ban in London school', ran a 2021 *Guardian* headline, whereas many non-linguists we talk to are very keen indeed on the idea of 'banning slang' in schools.

And Deborah Cameron is not the only one to realise that, for whatever reason, academic linguists have largely failed to cut through on this question. A lot of linguists, or at least a lot of the ones who engage with public policy and debate, find that they spend a good deal of their time battling received ideas. This was a 2021 tweet by sociolinguist Rob Drummond – someone who spends a lot of time stressing the value of research into the way young people speak:

> We know that terms like 'accent reduction', 'proper grammar' and 'correct English' are meaningless, damaging, and discriminatory. But the fact that they are still used and widely understood means we (linguists/educators) need to do better at explaining why this is the case.

This is quite right, and we are going to try to do our bit by exploring some of these issues in the next couple of chapters. It is tempting, though, to speculate for a moment on why linguists and the public (and education ministers!) so often seem to be talking at cross-purposes. Perhaps it is just an inevitable result of the fact that, unlike the subjects of some other fields of academic study, language has a central place in everyone's conscious lives – so everyone has formed their own opinions about it. That is to say, you might not have an opinion about molecular biology, or calculus, or The War of the Spanish Succession, but you've been using language pretty much all your life (and listening to lots of other people using it, too), you've developed views on it, and you're likely to feel that you have a right to say what you think about it. But this practical and emotional engagement with language is not often matched by genuine *knowledge* about it. Few people have really studied language to any great degree; even language teachers don't need to have any training in linguistics; and general public knowledge of the basics of linguistics hovers between minimal and non-existent.

1.5 About this book

1.5.1 What we're trying to do

The broad purpose of this book, then, is to try to build some much-needed bridges between academic linguistics and day-to-day school life. To some extent at least, this means engaging in political arguments, for, as the educational linguist Ian Cushing has rightly noted, 'politicians have resisted much insight and expertise from linguists',[11] and in the end it is politicians who are responsible for setting the terms of the debate; but it is the situation on the ground that we are primarily concerned with. Decisions about language matters are taken all the time in schools. Some are relatively minor, or seem to be so – should a child who reads the word *water* as 'wa'er' be corrected when reading out loud? Others are big and have serious consequences: which foreign languages should be offered at GCSE and A level, and why? Do we embrace the concept of the 'word gap', or is it a red herring (or worse)? Should we join forces with volunteers in the local community to offer 'heritage' language teaching? And some decisions are so fundamental that they set the tone for how the school is run, how it engages with its local community, and what is expected of its pupils. For example, should we ban 'street talk' and slang, and insist on Standard English at all times? Should we follow the enthusiastic advice of various academy heads and ministers for education and for school standards, and embrace the strict language regime laid down by the American educationalist Doug Lemov in his influential *Teach Like A Champion* book?

In discussing these and other issues from a language awareness perspective, using the insights that the broad discipline of linguistics offers, we want to help teachers, school management teams and perhaps even parents to make better – that is, better *informed* – language decisions. Specifically, we want:

1. to help teachers and school management teams develop their thinking about language use and language issues along reasoned, evidence-based lines, using the frameworks offered by linguistics and sociolinguistics.

2. to encourage and exemplify school-level and classroom-level policy and practice that will help students to be more confident and capable users of language, and help teachers to be more confident about their language choices.

3. to argue for an increased role for language awareness in teacher education and professional development.

Underlying this is our long-standing conviction that the classroom and the school should function as a natural site for noticing and talking about language, and for exploring language behaviour in all its facets. We are keen to boost awareness of language issues at every level in schools: apart from anything else, we really do think that the 'every teacher a language teacher' slogan is one which should be taken seriously, and that language is the responsibility of all. But let us point out that what we are emphatically *not* trying to do is blame teachers for the current low level of language awareness in most schools. Rather, we want to argue for a much wider application of the insights of linguistics throughout the school system, as well as in teacher education and subsequent professional development, and we recognise that this will need to involve a change in thinking (and perhaps funding?) at the government level.

One last thing that we're not trying to do. While we might mention them in passing, we won't comment in any detail on particular matters involving UK minority languages such as Gaelic, Welsh, or British Sign Language. We regard these as specialised cases, requiring specialist knowledge and professional experience that we don't pretend to have. We do, though, hope very much that readers who are professionally or personally involved in these language communities will find much in this book that they are able to relate to their own experience and context.

1.5.2 About us

There have been a good number of books written about language awareness at school in recent years. However, most of them focus, reasonably enough, on specific applications of linguistics to classroom teaching, and don't set out to address the broader range of language issues; and they don't often set out explicitly to combine the viewpoints of an academic linguist and a practising teacher. Since that is what we have tried to do in this book, we should probably tell the reader a little about the relevant parts of our backgrounds.

Tim is a writer and lecturer specialising in languages and applied linguistics, with a focus on linguistics in education. He has a PhD in applied linguistics and is a PGCE-qualified teacher of TESOL and MFL. He has been a classroom language teacher and university linguistics lecturer in various countries, a language teacher trainer and consultant, and director of an MA TESOL programme at a UK university. For the last few years he has worked mainly in universities in Colombia and China as well as the UK. He is the author (with Fiona English) of the books *Why Do Linguistics?* (2015, second edition 2023) and *Rethinking TESOL in Diverse Global Settings* (2019), both published by Bloomsbury.

Steve is Head of English at a large secondary school on the south coast of England, where he teaches Key Stages 3 and 4 as well as A Level. Having taught A Level English Literature and English Language and Literature, he now specialises in A Level English Language. He contributed a chapter on sentence-level analysis to the edited collection *Teaching A Level English Language and Literature 16–19* (Routledge, 2021). His first experience of teaching was as an EFL teacher in Peru and Oxfordshire, but he didn't go into mainstream teaching until he qualified as an English teacher in 2004, having spent several years working in Latin America and the UK in journalism and tourism.

We first met as EFL teachers at the splendidly named William Shakespeare Institute of English in Lima, Peru, in the 1980s. We were straight out of university, had never received any substantial training in teaching English, and had barely a word of Spanish between us. But we were seriously interested in language and languages. Over the following decades, we found ourselves continually talking about language and linguistics, and, more recently, about specific language issues in education. In the end, given that no one else appeared to have written that book that we thought would be so useful – the one where a linguistics academic and a secondary school teacher get together to share their perspectives and show how linguistics can inform policy and practice right across the school – it seemed a natural step to just write it ourselves.

One point about terminology. There's an irritating thing that happens every so often on social media sites where people gather to discuss linguistics. Someone (it's usually a youngish linguistics postgraduate) will say something along the lines of: 'Don't you hate it when you tell people you're a linguist, and they ask you how many languages you speak?' Others then chime in with things like, 'omg yes, it's so predictable! Why don't people understand what we do?' This reaction is really rather unreasonable. In normal, everyday English, 'linguist' does indeed describe a person who happens to speak several languages, or has studied several languages. 'How many languages do you speak?' is a perfectly sensible and understandable question to ask such a person. It is hardly the fault of the general public that people who study the discipline of linguistics – and who might actually be monolingual, of course – decided at some point that they would also use that word to describe themselves. The (in our view more accurate!) term 'linguistician' exists, and was used at various points during the twentieth century; but it has never had wide acceptance, and now sounds irredeemably clunky and old-fashioned. So we are stuck with 'linguist', and throughout this book, we use the word to mean someone who does linguistics, usually at a university.

1.5.3 Who we're writing for

As we mentioned earlier, we hope that this book will prove useful for many of those working in schools or associated with schools – from classroom teachers and school management teams to governors, policy makers at all levels and even some parents. So we'd like to make it clear at the outset that this is not intended to be an 'academic' book, and we are not writing for professional academics (though it is certainly informed by academic principles, and we hope that at least some academics will read it). With that in mind, wherever possible we have tried to avoid the heavier kind of academic style, and to keep academic jargon to a minimum when discussing practice and, especially, theory. That said, we happily and unapologetically use terms from linguistics and sociolinguistics where appropriate – register, discourse, sociolect, for example – for the simple reason that they are extraordinarily helpful for explaining and understanding how language works. We explain the terms when they first crop up, and we have provided a short glossary, too, for ease of reference.

By the same token, we have tried to keep the number of references to a minimum, but sometimes they are necessary, helpful or both. We have, though, avoided the in-text referencing customary in many academic disciplines, and opted instead for endnotes, so as to avoid cluttering up the text and distracting the reader.

1.5.4 Language awareness, and what we take it to mean

Language awareness can admittedly be a slightly slippery concept to grasp. It's not exactly a discipline in itself. Rather, it's an area of study or approach within applied linguistics which looks at what people actually know or think about language. Hence it can be applicable to fields of activity like translation, say, or workplace communication: but naturally, much of it focuses on the educational sphere, and particularly on the field of second or foreign language learning. So research in it quite often involves things like investigating the extent to which second language learners use their explicit knowledge of language as a system (e.g. their knowledge of how grammar works) to help them acquire aspects of the target language that they are studying.

But we want to widen our focus well beyond what happens in actual teaching, or in classrooms, and take the development of language awareness as a broad remit. For the purposes of this book, then, we have chosen to interpret language awareness at school in the widest sense: as a way of *thinking about school language issues through a linguistically informed lens*. We conceive of it as a means of incorporating the insights of linguistics not only into language teaching, but also into teaching in the sciences and other subjects, school management and school language policy, teacher training and professional development, and national educational policy making. And so we look not just at language across the curriculum, but at how whole-school language policy is developed, how Standard English is positioned and promoted, how foreign and 'community' languages are treated, and so on.

So to be clear – when we say awareness of language, we're not just talking about awareness of literacy – which most schools tend to already be on top of these days, with literacy coordinators and literacy strategies and the like – we're talking about *language* in the broadest terms. We will likewise interpret the term 'linguistics' in a broad sense – we're not going to be talking about arcane theoretical linguistics of the Chomskyan variety. This is important, for it is by adopting a wide-ranging view of what the field of linguistics encompasses that teachers will find it of most practical use to them. Like Marcello Giovanelli and Dan Clayton in their book *Knowing About Language*, we use the term linguistics 'to refer to all aspects of the field covering language as a system, the study of its users, and as an underlying set of principles of thinking about communication and the construction of meaning'.[12] And like them, we would certainly invite all teachers to think of themselves as being in some way applied linguists, people who use the insights of linguistics to illuminate real-world issues and problems.

Lexicographer of slang Jonathon Green once mused that: 'The problem with linguistics, other than for its devotees, is that it is, dare one suggest, not easily accessible.' We hope to show that that's not necessarily the case.

1.5.5 How we've laid the book out

The central part of the book – excluding this introductory chapter and a concluding one – falls broadly into two halves. In the first half, 'Policy and Practice' (Chapters 2 to 4), we take a fairly wide-ranging look at how schools approach language issues, starting with what linguistic foundations policy needs to rest on in order to be effective and moving on to show what a language-aware policy actually looks like at the level of classroom practice. In the second half, 'Language as Subject' (Chapters 5 to 7), we focus on how language is treated from the perspective of the different language-based disciplines, first discussing English (or Englishes, as we should perhaps call it) and then turning to modern foreign languages, including so-called community or heritage languages.

Chapter 2, 'What people get wrong about language', discusses the question of standard language, dialect and Standard English in some detail, using it as an example of how the kind of ignorance or confusion about language that we have already mentioned (at 1.2 and 1.3 above) can lead to bad policy making, which in turn leads to poor outcomes for students – and especially the less socially privileged ones. Chapters 3 and 4 take currently influential notions such as cultural capital, the 'language gap' and the 'word gap', and consider them from a linguistics point of view. We argue that tackling the so-called 'word gap', for example, is insufficient and misplaced if the aim is to improve students' literacy and articulacy. Rather than focusing simply on *words*, teachers' efforts might be better directed towards developing students' awareness of how academic discourses work as a whole, involving considerations of register (including subject-specific registers), appropriacy to context, and the matching of communicative resources to desired communicative outcomes. Chapter 4 contains multiple examples of what this approach might actually look like at the classroom level, and across different subjects.

Moving to the second part of the book, Chapter 5, 'What we teach when we teach English', considers the issue of 'English' from first principles: what exactly is this subject English, what does it consist of, how has it developed historically, and what is it that English teachers actually do? We suggest that one way of drawing together the disparate strands of a very amorphous and multifaceted subject is to think of language awareness as a common, unifying theme. We then consider how such an approach can be squared with the 'learning journey' of children through the National Curriculum for English as it exists at present. The next two chapters are entirely devoted to the question of foreign language learning and teaching. In the first of them, Chapter 6, we address the decline in take-up of MFLs over a long period, and return to a sociolinguistically informed drawing board to establish why it is so important to promote language learning, and how students and their parents might be better encouraged to engage with the whole project. In the complementary Chapter 7, we use the insights of academic linguistics, and in particular those of sociolinguistics and second language acquisition, to develop frameworks for making decisions on such matters as, for example, which language(s) a school should offer, and how the issue of 'early' or primary language teaching might best be approached. In the final, practical Chapter 8, by way of a conclusion, we lay out how, in our opinion, language awareness might be built into the existing school system at classroom, school and national levels. At the end you will find a (handy, we hope) glossary of terms related to language and linguistics.

1.6 To sum up

As we suggested at 1.3.2 above in the context of the 'zero tolerance' school in Middlesbrough, the value of adopting a linguistics lens lies primarily in the fact that perceived language problems can in this way be turned into learning opportunities.

This even applies to seemingly intractable problems such as the historical divide between English literature and language (and the confusion it causes), the decline in take-up of foreign languages, or the existence of a supposed 'word gap' among disadvantaged pupils. Such things move into clearer focus and are more effectively tackled when teachers and schools take a linguistically informed approach to thinking about language issues. And then there is the whole question of Standard English, non-standard dialects, 'street' speech and slang, where we started this chapter. Doug Lemov has insisted in *Teach Like A Champion* that school is not the 'time and place in which to engage [pupils] in a broader sociological discourse on dialect'.[13] But surely school is precisely *the* time and place! Pupils need to have these discussions. Teachers and management teams need to have these discussions, too.

We are of the opinion that, given the foundation provided by sound linguistic and sociolinguistic knowledge, schools could do better. The potential benefits are multiple: more self-assured young people, confident and informed about the way they express themselves in different contexts; more focused and engaging MFL delivery; better integrated language development across the curriculum; better relations with parents and the local community; a more welcoming environment which values staff and student linguistic repertoires… we could go on.

And that's why we're talking about language.

Notes

1 https://educationandsociety.wordpress.com/2013/03/03/nowt-banned-from-middlesbrough-school/
2 English, F. & Marr, T. (2015, 2nd edition 2023), *Why Do Linguistics?* London & New York: Bloomsbury.
3 https://www.complex.com/life/ark-all-saints-bans-students-from-using-filler-slang
4 https://www.hollandparkeducation.com/blog/public-school-slang/. For non-British readers, we should perhaps clarify that the term 'public school', in England especially, refers not to a state-run school, but to one of a small number of expensive fee-paying, selective, private boarding schools traditionally associated with the education of the upper classes.
5 *Daily Telegraph*, 24 October 2018.
6 *The Guardian*, 15 November 2013.
7 https://www.dailymail.co.uk/news/article-2791261/ban-black-country-slang-improved-reading-writing-claims-controversial-primary-school-sparked-anger-pulling-pupils-local-dialect.html
8 https://www.asianage.com/newsmakers/210519/meet-8-yr-old-polyglot-from-chennai-can-read-and-write-over-106-languages.html
9 https://www.independent.co.uk/news/uk/home-news/teacher-told-to-sound-less-northern-after-southern-ofsted-inspection-8947332.html
10 https://www.theguardian.com/education/2014/nov/28/community-languages-uk-young-attitudes
11 In Cushing, I. (2020), 'The policy and policing of language in schools'. *Language in Society* 49 (3): 425–450.
12 London: Routledge 2016, p. 4.
13 Lemov, D. (2010), *Teach Like A Champion: 49 Techniques That Put Students On The Right Path To College.* San Francisco: Jossey-Bass, p. 48.

PART I
Policy and practice

2 What people get wrong about language

2.1 Introduction: from language attitudes to language policy

In a primary school in the south of England, a teaching assistant is listening to a child read aloud from a book. The child comes to the word 'bottle', and produces a glottal stop for the /t/ sound, as is common in the local area. 'Read it properly!' says the TA, with an encouraging smile. But what does she mean? Is she actually helping the child's language and literacy development – or hindering it?

Language-related questions like this one (witnessed by Steve) come up every day in schools. As we said in the last chapter, this book aims to help you find good answers to them, by laying out the fundamental linguistic principles we all need to know in order to think these issues through. By the end of this chapter, the way to approach this particular problem should, we hope, be clear. So we'll return to it then. In the meantime, what we're going to argue in this chapter is that whole-school language policies can be a hugely effective tool for students' learning and development – *but only as long as those policies are based on solid linguistic understanding*. Research has shown that most trainee teachers' formal linguistic knowledge is low – and yes, by the way, that does include most English and even quite a lot of foreign language specialists.

There's a broader issue in play here, too. School policies are informed by attitudes. If you say 'students must answer in complete sentences only', or 'only Standard English must be used in the classroom', what view of language – and therefore of the students' language – does this imply? Where do these attitudes come from, and how are they spread? We will argue that entrenched language attitudes are often based on simple misunderstandings about how language works: misunderstandings that are never put right because too many schools don't teach about language – and so the cycle continues. We think that one way to help break this cycle is by encouraging a linguistically informed, language-aware school at all

DOI: 10.4324/9781003201281-3

levels, from reception desk to classroom to head teacher's office. And in this chapter, we want to establish some of the basic linguistic principles which school management teams need to take into account in developing effective language policies.

2.2 What exactly is 'Standard English' – and what is it not?

STANDARD ENGLISH: A widely used term that resists easy definition but is used as if most educated people nonetheless know precisely what it refers to.

Tom McArthur in the *Oxford Companion to the English Language* (1992)

When it comes to matters of language, many people – most people, in fact, including many teachers and school managers, not to mention politicians – appear to be working at the level of received ideas which might be based on nothing more than prejudice and personal opinion. Following on from our discussion in Chapter 1, there's an absolutely fundamental issue here that we have to get into sooner or later; and it might as well be now, because it is one of the things that most divide linguists from government and other laypeople. It is, of course, the currently hot topic of Standard English, what it is, what it isn't, and whether or how its use should be mandated in schools. What we intend to do first is to discuss how 'standard' languages are understood from a linguistics perspective.

Let us acknowledge immediately that this is a highly politicised area, and always has been. Readers of more mature years might remember the fuss in the 1980s and 1990s surrounding the books of maverick academic John Honey, which had in-your-face titles like *The Story of Standard English and Its Enemies* and *Does Accent Matter?* The debate has had something of a resurgence in recent times, as successive governments post-2010 have put renewed emphasis on the use of Standard English at school. Some academic linguists suspect that the imposition of what they refer to as a 'standard language ideology' is a means of placing a conservative, traditional stamp on every classroom in the country. It has even been argued that the insistence on Standard English being used in schools is a way of maintaining a class-based, even a specifically 'white' English; that its supposed neutrality is not neutrality at all, but in the words of Ian Cushing, a way of masking 'the structural power relations that are embedded in language'.[1]

The same writer has noted that while the term 'Standard English' appears 16 times in the DfE's 2014 primary national curriculum framework document and 13 times in the secondary equivalent, these crucial documents do not offer an up-front definition of it.[2] Now, to be fair, there is an entry for Standard English in the glossary which accompanies these documents on the official website (see Figure 2.1), which Cushing reproduces.[3] While the definition given there is admittedly a pretty scanty one ('Standard English can be recognised by the use of a very small range of forms... It is the variety of English which is used, with only minor variations, as a major world language'), there is one aspect of it which is admirably

Standard English	Standard English can be recognised by the use of a very small range of forms such as *those books, I did it* and *I wasn't doing anything* (rather than their non-Standard equivalents); it is not limited to any particular accent. It is the variety of English which is used, with only minor	*I did it because they were not willing to undertake any more work on those houses.* [formal Standard English] *I did it cos they wouldn't do any more work on those houses.* [casual Standard English]

15

English – Glossary

Term	Guidance	Example
	variation, as a major world language. Some people use Standard English all the time, in all situations from the most casual to the most formal, so it covers most registers. The aim of the national curriculum is that everyone should be able to use Standard English as needed in writing and in relatively formal speaking.	*I done it cos they wouldn't do no more work on them houses.* [casual non-Standard English]

Figure 2.1 DfE National Curriculum framework document (Glossary).

clear-sighted. This is that it recognises explicitly that a stretch of speech such as *I did it cos they wouldn't do any more work on those houses* is in every way as standard as *I did it because they were not willing to undertake any more work on those houses*. One is casual Standard English, the other is more formal Standard English – but they are certainly both standard. You could even call someone a *fucking bastard* and it would still be Standard English! (Though it would be low register, of course – not to mention most impolite.) All too often, lay people, and even teachers, equate standardness automatically with formal register. This is a misunderstanding which, as we shall see, can muddy the waters and confuse students when they are learning about the distance between their natural, home language and the 'Standard English' that they are expected to use in some or even all school contexts. Speaking standardly does not have to mean speaking formally.

And indeed, 'Standard English' is one of those terms which most laypeople tend to think they have a fair idea about, while linguists argue and debate endlessly about how to define it. They even argue about whether it can be said to exist at all, hence the slightly prissy scare quotes that they sometimes like to accompany it with. Certainly it becomes a rather hazy notion, even for non-linguists, when you begin to dig deeper into it. In the public mind, the idea of Standard English often gets mixed up with a standard *accent*, hence what is known loosely as Queen's English or BBC English or sometimes Oxford English, which all refer to a kind of ill-defined combination of standardised grammar and the way of speaking known as Received Pronunciation (RP). And, of course, despite the high visibility and historic prestige of the RP accent, very few people actually speak it – less than 5 per cent of the UK population, in fact, according to linguist James Milroy – though it's true that those few people do tend to wield a disproportionate amount of power and influence.

But let's leave the question of pronunciation and accent aside for now, and stick with the idea of Standard English as – basically – a substantially standardised set of grammar rules and a common core of vocabulary. So what's the problem with it? Well, the problem is that virtually all linguists (and historians, for that matter) would agree that standard languages are not simply handed down from above, as if on stone tablets. They are a product of history – of social and political forces. So when it is simply asserted (on page 10 of the primary national curriculum framework document that we mentioned just now) that schoolchildren 'should be taught the correct use of grammar', and when, in the same document, speaking 'with an increasing command of Standard English' is associated with speaking clearly and even thinking clearly, this rather begs the question. *Why* is this particular form of speaking and writing considered to be more correct and even clearer than others? Where did its special status come from? Who decided, and on what grounds? In official documents as in much public debate, it is often simply assumed that 'correct grammar' is no more than 'the grammar of Standard English'.

But it isn't.

2.2.1 Isn't 'Standard English' just another way of saying 'proper English'?

Here is the opening line of an article called 'What Is Standard English?', from a website called 'The School Run', plucked at random from a range of similar websites, all of which offer support and guidance to parents of schoolchildren[4]:

> Standard English is accepted as the 'correct' form of English, used in formal speaking or writing.

We'll look more closely at the advice offered by this website in a moment. But first let's deal with this big claim: that Standard English 'is accepted as the correct form of English'. Now, there's a glaringly obvious question here, as we have already indicated: accepted by whom, exactly? But even if we ignore that question for the time being, this definition still manages to misunderstand and misrepresent entirely the real relationship between 'correct' English and Standard English – for they are really not the same thing.

How so? Well, one way to think about this relationship is to consider different kinds of 'incorrectness', or different degrees of distance from the standard. If I were to present you with an utterance such as:

> Uply only assuming agains the at taken

then you would rightly call it gibberish. For one thing, it doesn't have any obvious meaning. However, that's not the main reason why we have to class it as unacceptable: sometimes we don't understand things that are said even by other speakers of the same language as us (do Nigerians always easily understand Geordies, or New Yorkers the English of New Delhi?). Linguistically speaking, the problem is that it doesn't have any recognisable *grammar*: that is to say, the words and even some of the constituent parts of the words don't fit together according to any system of rules that we know of.

Now have a look at this one:

Blue car belong to lady over there

Most linguists (though perhaps not all) would also agree that this is ungrammatical and therefore unacceptable. It's perfectly comprehensible, of course – but again, that's not the main point. What is important is that it doesn't follow the rules of any native speaker's variety of English. It feels like a decent attempt by a non-native speaker to make themselves understood without knowing too many of the systematic, established grammar rules of English. You can imagine it being said by, for instance, a speaker of Russian or Polish, or another Slavic language which doesn't use definite or indefinite articles. Now, how about this third and last one?

I weren't right happy about that

This, as you've probably noticed, is something quite different to the other two. Granted, it's still not Standard English, but *I weren't right happy about that* is demonstrably rule-governed – that is, it conforms to a regular, predictable, systematic grammar. To be specific, it follows the grammatical rules of a widespread northern English dialect,[5] which most British people at least will have come across at some point. In this dialect (think for example of Yorkshire and Lancashire), the first, second and third persons of the past tense of 'to be' are all formed with *were* in both singular and plural: so we have *I were, she were, it were, we were* and so on. The chorus of a song by folk singer Keith Hancock from some decades back will give you the flavour of it:

Ee, when I were a lad, the times they were bad,
But not quite as bad as when me dad were a lad.
When me dad were a lad, it were nearly as bad
As when me dad's dad were a lad.

Thanks for that, Keith.

It's interesting to note by the way that the standard, modern German for *I was* and *she/he was* are *ich war* and *sie/er war* – so you can see very clearly that those northern English words come from the same root, or are 'cognates', in the linguistic jargon; and indeed, all forms of English and German share a common Germanic ancestor. As for *right happy*, well, a common intensifier for adjectives in this northern English dialect is not *very*, but *right*. Once upon a time this was perfectly acceptable formal English, too, and you can see the historical trace of it in the now archaic-sounding 'right royal' or 'the Right Honourable Member for Macclesfield'.

So from a linguistics point of view, *I weren't right happy* is entirely grammatical! It is 'proper English', just as the closely related German is proper, in fact *standard* German. It is in every way acceptable and correctly formed, because for linguists, a sentence or utterance is grammatical if it obeys the rules of a native-speaker variety of a language, not just if it obeys the rules of the standard variety of a language. This is not at all to say that children should not learn how to use Standard English (we think they certainly should). Nor is it to say that 'anything goes' or that native speakers never make errors. It is simply to make the point that when a community of native speakers say something habitually and systematically, it's not a mistake, and it's not ungrammatical. Dialectal variation is something that is communally agreed upon, albeit in a fuzzy and unconscious kind of way; it has always existed, and it continues to exist even where there also exists a formal standard. It existed long *before* there was ever a 'standard'.

This leads us straight to our next, large point. The dominance of the formal standard has nothing to do with the language itself: it's entirely down to historical and political factors. That is, there is nothing linguistically special about the variant of English we call Standard English, and *I was* is not in any way better, clearer, more regular or more correct than *I were*. It's just that it has acquired prestige and authority, because it happens to be part of the London/east Midlands variety of English that gradually became established as Standard English from late medieval times, as the speakers of that variety established their political dominance. If history had turned out differently, and York rather than London had become the capital of England, the elites who spoke the northern dialect would no doubt have insisted on enthroning *their* own style of speech as the standard, and *I weren't right happy* would now be regarded as correct, while *I wasn't very happy* would be relegated to the status of a quaint or sub-standard dialectal usage. This is why many critical linguists describe the idea that certain types of language are 'better' or 'worse' or even more 'appropriate' for certain things as a 'constructed notion'. Standard languages are standards for *social* reasons, not linguistic ones!

It's true that most academic linguists in the UK, like most UK academics in general, to be honest, tend to lean leftwards politically. But it's very important to understand that what we have just said about standard languages isn't a politically motivated claim or an ivory tower academic theory, put about by what the tabloids used to call 'trendy lefties'. It doesn't change according to whether you are a left-wing linguist or a right-wing one, or something in between. It's just a linguistic fact, as basic and uncontroversial for those who study language professionally as the composition of the atom is to those who study physics. Of course, broadly speaking, a more conservative-minded linguist might be more in favour of the widespread teaching and use of Standard English in schools, and a less conservative-minded one less so. But being language professionals, they would both accept without a murmur that standards are standards for historical and political reasons, not because they are somehow the most 'correct' or the 'best' or the 'clearest' form of the language. And, of course, standards *change* over time. The *History of the English Language* points out that, even though many speakers believe in the existence of a fixed norm, '[t]o think that language could be fixed in the same way as, say, the metre or shoe sizes… is an illusion.'[6] Or as Dr Amanda Cole of Essex University pithily put it in a 2021 article for the website *The Conversation*: 'What we think of as correct English is like a yardstick in quicksand.'

All of this helps explain why linguists are driven to howls of rage, or at the very least muffled sobs, when well-meaning sources such as 'The School Run' website kick off their advice for parents on the subject of Standard English. They begin with a series of blithe assertions which manage to be wrong at almost every stage. And again, let's be clear: when we say wrong, we don't mean 'we disagree with this', we really do mean *wrong*. As in, they are misleading parents badly about the idea of standard language – what it is and how it works – and in the process sowing confusion among children, too. Let's go back to the website:

> In primary school children are expected to learn to write according to the rules of Standard English. Standard English may also be referred to as 'correct' English. It follows grammatical rules like subject-verb agreement and the correct use of verb tenses or pronouns.

There then follows a series of examples of standard versus non-standard usage, like these:

> Non-standard English: They ain't got nothing
> Standard English: They haven't got anything
> Non-standard English: We was there yesterday
> Standard English: We were there yesterday

Bearing in mind what we said before about the relation between Standard English and other varieties, it should now be obvious why this is so misleading. To state that Standard English 'follows grammatical rules' implies that dialectal forms somehow don't. But this shows a dire lack of understanding of how language works. *All* native speaker varieties of language have grammatical rules, which all the speakers of that variety intuitively know and understand – otherwise, how on earth could they understand each other? If you could use any old words and word endings you liked, in any old order, every conversation would be potential chaos! But *those grammatical rules are not necessarily the same as the rules of Standard English*. People who say *I were* are not speaking randomly, or mistakenly, or confusedly, or unclearly. They are following the established, consistent grammatical rules of their dialect, in exactly the same way that speakers using the standard dialect would say *I was*. (And yes, Standard English is a dialect, though a socially privileged one.) Native speakers of any language don't repeatedly happen upon the 'wrong' words – they use these forms predictably and systematically. So non-standard does not equal ungrammatical, as this 2021 tweet by actors' accent and dialect coach Mary Howland illustrates:

> 'Standard' is not the same as 'correct', any more than International Klein Blue or Pantone 15-4020 is a 'correct' blue – it's just an agreed reference point to measure all other blues (including greens and purples) against. A starting point, not necessarily an end point.

Of course, many linguists would further argue that the standard is not even really an 'agreed' reference point – for who was ever consulted about it? Rather, it's a reference point that has emerged from historical struggles for power and influence – and, as we have just noted, it is subject to change. But Mary's point is well taken: 'standard' is really, really not a synonym for 'correct'!

2.2.2 'Model competent speech': classroom and school-level approaches to non-standard language

So you can imagine where this is going. When the government itself, in the form of the official 2013 DfE guidelines for GCSE English Language, airily instructs that children should be taught to 'use grammar correctly' and 'write grammatically correct sentences', it naturally drives linguists to distraction. In the Spelling, Punctuation and Grammar (SPaG) test, which is taken at Key Stage 2 (Year 6) of primary school, pupils are invited to label 'I were' as grammatically incorrect, but, as we have just noted, it would be correct for many speakers from the north of England. It's not incorrect at all, it's just not *standard*. When fundamental misunderstanding about how language works and what 'correct' grammar is starts right from the top, it is scarcely a surprise that some schools – not all, thankfully – reproduce this misunderstanding at whole-school and classroom level. Hence the jarringly ill-expressed advice that teachers should 'model accurate talk by addressing grammatical errors' (as if non-standard grammar was 'inaccurate' in some mysterious way!) and 'model competent speech', by which, of course, they mean Standard English.[7] Are they really suggesting that children's natural dialectal forms are *errors*? Inaccurate, incompetent ways of speaking? Well, yes – it appears that they are.

It is from this kind of government advice, unfortunately, that many websites and other sources of information for parents and teachers take their cue. And so the damaging misunderstanding spreads outwards, as language guidance is dispensed with confidence by people who know next to nothing about language, but have evidently amassed ample stocks of language-related prejudices and assumptions.

We could try and help out a little by rewriting the website's badly mistaken advice from a more linguistically informed point of view. Let's have a go.

Standard English is the name given to a substantially regularised variety of English which over time has come to be regarded as broadly acceptable and understood wherever English is used. It is the form most often associated with educated or formal speaking or writing – though it can be spoken in any accent, and the spoken and written forms are not always identical.

We then might give a little more detailed guidance, like this:

The grammatical rules of Standard English may well differ from the rules of regional dialects and other non-standard forms of the language which children use at home with their families and in the peer groups they identify with. In primary school children should learn to write and speak according to the rules of Standard English where appropriate, and begin to develop a sense of when such writing or speaking is appropriate.[8]

As you can see, we've removed the idea of 'correct' here, not because we're trying to make a political point (we're not) but because it just doesn't help. It doesn't help children understand the idea of register – that is to say, of the difference between how they might speak in everyday contexts and how they might be expected to write and speak in more formal or specialised contexts. And it further doesn't help because it has the effect of marginalising and demeaning children's natural speech, for no good reason. In fact, on the basis of government guidance (in the Teachers' Standards document) you as a teacher can find yourself required to treat your students' way of speaking as simply wrong, whether you believe this to be the case or not. As Ian Cushing has described in detail, some schools really do enforce this approach, demanding that Standard English be used at all times, that students using non-standard language be 'corrected' without exception, and that posters pointing out errors (i.e. non-standard language) be on display in all classrooms.

Again, let's be clear: instructions like these could *only* have been written by someone who doesn't understand what a standard language is, or how grammar works. This is perhaps an inevitable outcome when governments prefer to act on their own linguistic and social prejudices rather than heed those who have linguistic knowledge and expertise. In 2011 the government undertook consultation on how English grammar should be taught within the National Curriculum – it's worth looking at the response submitted by the Committee for Linguistics in Education (CLiE), who know a thing or two about this topic. The CLiE started off by pointing out that analysing grammar 'is not the same as 'teaching "correct" grammar, which consists of a rather arbitrary list of do's and don'ts' and emphasised that '"teaching grammar", in our sense, is not about split infinitives and double negatives, but about the structure of words and sentences'. Crucially, they called for systematic education *about* grammar, rather than the simple imposition of the standard:

> Grammatical analysis is as relevant to casual non-standard speech as it is to formal standard writing: *I ain't saying nothing* has just as much grammatical structure as *I am not saying anything*, and exploring the differences should be an important part of education.

And while they were quite explicit about the need to teach Standard English, they placed such teaching firmly in its proper context:

> We accept the need for children to learn Standard English and the 'etiquette' of formal writing and speaking, but this is only a small part of the language development that takes place during the school years.[9]

The advice was not taken, which is a great pity, because this is an eminently sensible and constructive response, as one would expect from an expert source like the CLiE. People who are genuinely interested in how language works and who genuinely care about students' all-round language development will always encourage analysis, discussion and comparison of standard and non-standard speech in the classroom. And why would they not? After all, which is most likely to help and motivate students to understand the differences between standard and non-standard ways of speaking – getting them to compare and analyse the two, or intimating to them that their own, their friends' and their parents' natural way of speaking is wrong and needs to be corrected, or excluded from the classroom?

The pivotal Bullock Report *A Language for Life* had already recognised the basic injustice of the latter approach back in 1975. A much-quoted section stated:

> No child can be expected to cast off the language and culture of the home as he [*sic*] crosses the school threshold.

And that approach is not only unjust, it's counter-productive. If you want students to understand the value of Standard English, they first need to understand what it is and what it isn't – then they can learn it, and learn *about* it, in an informed manner, rather than experiencing it as an imposition, a context-free diktat from above.

Seen in this light, it would seem bizarre to oblige young people to always use Standard English, regardless of the context, of appropriacy, and of how they would normally express themselves and forge their own linguistic identities (and you'll remember we talked about local dialects in Chapter 1). And yet in too many places, this is precisely what happens. The literacy and oracy policy of one school in Leeds, singled out for particular praise by a campaigning Minister for Schools, stipulates that 'students are expected to speak in full sentences, using standard English at all times'.[10]

Which brings us rather neatly on to another controversial subject.

2.3 Speaking in full sentences

As has been clear for some time from the debates carried on via social media and in the pages of the TES and other publications, an increasing number of schools have policies in place which require their students to 'speak in full sentences'. In this they have often had enthusiastic government backing, as we have just seen, buoyed by the popularity in some circles of Doug Lemov's book *Teach Like A Champion*; but it is fair to say that there has also been much criticism of the notion from more linguistically aware teachers and commentators. In Chapter 3 we are going to look in some detail at how language policies play out at classroom level. But for the moment, and in partial preparation for that, let's look at the particular question of 'full sentences' from a linguistics point of view, and see if we can establish some basic principles that will help us understand the surrounding issues better.

We'll begin with a fact of linguistic life which might seem surprising, but which serves to put all the controversy into context: *there isn't really any such thing as a spoken sentence*. If you look through the academic literature, there is a fair amount of consensus about the matter. Without wishing to bombard you, here's a sample of what some respected sources have to say about it. The authors of *Exploring Grammar in Context* regard sentences in speech as 'problematic'.[11] The *Longman Grammar of Spoken and Written English* goes further and considers the whole concept of sentences debatable – even in writing! – and hence tends to avoid the word 'sentence' altogether, focusing instead on describing clauses, in both spoken and written language.[12] The legendary M. A. K. Halliday, meanwhile – perhaps the most influential linguist the UK has ever produced – states firmly that when he uses 'sentence', it 'refers only to units of orthography'.[13]

This is pretty clear. Sentences are not a natural unit of language. They are an idea borrowed from the technical apparatus of *writing*, which is, of course, a relatively recent invention. Nobody thought of 'speaking in complete sentences' before writing systems were developed. When we speak, we naturally speak in units of meaning, signalled in part by the stress and intonation we use. These units might coincide with the way the same words would be written down as sentences, or they might not. And there are many other ways in which speech differs systematically from writing. When we speak we use a lot of redundancy – that is, we repeat things, we say the same thing two or three different ways. We hesitate and *um* and *ah*, we make false starts and recast what we want to say; we correct ourselves, we make small errors which go largely unnoticed, we are interrupted, we fail to finish and leave things hanging; we monitor the person we are speaking to in order to check that we are being understood; we change and adapt what we say according to clues from context. All of these things are entirely natural, and are part and parcel of the intensely social and co-operative system that is human spoken interaction.

Even formal speech, unless it takes the extreme form of reading aloud from a prepared script, is very much less structured than formal writing – and rather differently structured, too. Here is a short extract from a university lecture on natural ecosystems, transcribed by a linguist. The (.) indicates a micro pause, the (..) a slightly longer pause, and the (…) an extended pause. It's worth noting that while the lecturer was horrified when he saw the transcript, in fact the lecture was a great success, came over as fluid and smooth, and was greatly appreciated by the audience.

> Now what I've (.) what I want you to imagine at the start (.) is a core community. (…) what I want us to imagine is a core community. (..) eventually. (.) and I'm going to talk about everything in relation to this core community. (…) that will be in a moment. (…) the key divisions. (.) er (.) the (.) the (..) of this formation. (..) um (.) of this classification. begins as follows.

Sentences are not how we speak. So the idea of getting people to 'speak in complete sentences' is essentially a category error. It conflates two quite different forms of language. It's a bit like getting a chimpanzee to dress up in clothes: it might be superficially striking, if that's your sort of thing, but it's unnatural, not to say awkward and uncomfortable. This is particularly so in the case of students responding to a teacher's question, something that at least one academy school group has insisted should always be done using a full sentence. In fact, a single word answer is very often entirely sufficient, appropriate and grammatical. The mistaken belief that there is something somehow incorrect about this was pinpointed and debunked by the notoriously strict grammarian Robert Lowth in his *Short Introduction to English Grammar*[14] – more than 250 years ago!

> Every Nominative case… belongs to some Verb, either expressed or implied: as in the answer to a Question: 'Who wrote this Book? Cicero.' that is, 'Cicero *wrote it.*'

There is really no justification for considering most short answers incomplete, unless you are mixing up the way people interact in the context of a co-operative face-to-face conversation with the way they write a structured academic essay. But people do mix these things up. One teacher, in a recent TES article entitled 'Why I insist on standard English in my classroom', conflates speaking with writing, and the question of Standard English with that of 'complete sentences':

> While spoken and written standard English is not exactly the same, there is a relationship between how students answer questions verbally [*sic*] and how

they translate this into writing. If not corrected, students will write how they speak when answering academic questions.

He goes on to explain in more detail why this 'correcting' of students' spoken English is necessary:

> If I allow them to answer verbally in non-standard English, I can usually find some of this translated into their written English when they write it down. I have found this issue minimised by asking students to answer verbal questions in full sentences. This allows them to model their answer to me before they write it down.[15]

So even while this teacher explicitly acknowledges that speaking and writing may differ, in explaining why he insists on pupils answering in complete sentences, he reveals that it is because he wants them to 'model' writing – that is, to speak as if they were writing. He goes on to suggest that 'It would seem counter-intuitive for me to allow students to speak non-standard English in my classroom, while expecting them to write academic essays in standard English'; and that 'Good oracy of standard English helps students to write better academic essays'.

There are at least two problems with this: first, it's actually *not* counter-intuitive, or shouldn't be – it is how language very often works. We say X in this way (which might be quite informal), and we write X in this way (which might be more formal). The crucial thing is that students should understand the difference. Second, even if one were to insist on standard English being spoken at all times, standard *speaking* ('good oracy of standard English') is again confused with formal *writing*, even though the teacher himself has just pointed out that they are not the same. Some linguists have suggested that there are in fact (at least) three levels of Standard English – the formal, the informal/mainstream, and the vernacular.[16] As we noted at Section 2.2 above, it is perfectly possible to speak informally – even to swear, if you must! – in Standard English. *Speech is not writing.* Even formal speech is not meant to be a reflection of writing, or writing spoken out loud (which is why skilled public speakers adjust their 'written' speeches to be more suitable for a listening audience). And by the same token, of course, writing is not speech, nor does it represent a higher model of language that speech should necessarily follow. It is a *technology*, developed in order to communicate things in a predominantly non-speechlike way.

The content of the National Curriculum reflects this basic confusion and misunderstanding. As has been repeatedly pointed out, it shows 'no distinction between spoken and written language, and little recognition of linguistic variation or the social value of regional forms'.[17] This helps explain, perhaps, why it is often said that working-class children don't pronounce words properly – by which is meant, presumably, that they don't pronounce words as they are written. But this is to misunderstand the nature of English spelling. Unlike in Spanish or Finnish or

Turkish, say, in English *nobody* systematically pronounces words exactly as they are written, because the writing system in English does not simply mirror the spoken word. So speakers of Received Pronunciation (RP) do not pronounce all words as they are spelt, either. For example, unlike most Americans, they don't pronounce the /r/ sounds in words like *doctor* or *partner* – so they sound a bit like 'doct-uh' (/'dɒktə/) and 'paht-nuh' (/'pɑːtnə/).[18] And, of course, absolutely no one argues on this account that middle-class RP-speakers are not pronouncing the words properly!

And so we see how the notion of 'speaking in complete sentences' is linked organically to a confusion between speaking and writing, and how both are rooted in a frustratingly widespread lack of language awareness. If the desired outcome is to help students write and speak in ways appropriate to context, then the solution to the whole problem lies in developing linguistically informed approaches to the teaching of literacy and oracy. It is not fair, accurate or helpful to tell students who use non-standard dialect forms that they are speaking wrongly, or to insist that everyone must use Standard English at all times. And it is certainly not helpful to impose a strange and unnatural 'full sentences only' rule which forces speech into the straitjacket of formal writing and casts normal spoken language behaviour as somehow incompetent or inadequate.

Linguistically aware teachers work with the grain of language, not against it.

2.4 Attitudes to speaking (or speakin')

In my first year at secondary school, I (Tim) remember being taken aside by a particular teacher and told quite aggressively and impatiently that I had an ugly and sloppy Yorkshire accent, which I would do well to get rid of. Now, you might think that this was par for the course for those days – schools in the 1970s were a bit more knockabout than would be considered acceptable now – but this was a school in Bradford, Yorkshire, and the teacher had a pretty strong Yorkshire accent himself. What was going on?

Accents tend to loom large in British people's lives, in one way or another. In big countries like Canada or the US, accents change only slowly over large geographical areas, while Russia and Poland, for example, are often said scarcely to have local accents at all. Accents in Italy or Korea commonly reveal a lot about a speaker's geographical background, but relatively little about their social class. But the history, geography and sociology of the British Isles have bequeathed to us in the UK a dense web of local accents, freighted not only with regional indicators but also with clues about class, education and social attitudes. And unfortunately, as we saw with the case of Standard English and grammar a little while back, standards of language awareness and linguistics knowledge are in general so low that there is no common terminology or set of generally-understood principles with which the question of accent can be properly discussed.

And so furious firestorms break out with some regularity in the press and on social media, like the one started by this tweet from Lord Digby Jones about a BBC TV Olympics commentator:

> Enough! I can't stand it anymore! Alex Scott spoils a good presentational job on the BBC Olympics Team with her very noticeable inability to pronounce her 'g's at the end of a word. Competitors are NOT taking part, Alex, in the fencin, rowin, boxin, kayakin, weightliftin & swimmin

Nor was poor Alex Scott the only one to attract Lord Jones's ire:

> She's hot on the heels of Beth Rigby at Sky [and] the Home Secretary for God's sake! Can't someone give these people elocution lessons? I fear that it may be aped by youngsters […] On behalf of the English Language… Help!

Again here we see the confusion between speaking and writing: Scott is being criticised for not pronouncing words as they are written, but as we have just noted, there is *no* systematic one-to-one correspondence between sounds and written symbols in English. That's just not the way the writing system of the language works. So is she really guilty of merely having a working-class or regional accent – that is, of not speaking RP? (She was brought up in Poplar, east London).

This kind of muddled thinking naturally extends into the school, too. The Teachers' Standards document calls for teachers to model 'articulate' speech – but as one team of sociolinguistic researchers ask in this regard, 'who decides what is, or is not, an articulate accent?'[19] Is 'articulate' maybe just code for RP? They note that mentors and senior staff have sometimes advised working-class teachers with strong regional accents to moderate the way they speak, making it more 'standard-like' and 'articulate' – which in practice means closer to RP. One internal school document, perhaps taking its lead similarly from the Teachers' Standards articulacy requirement, demanded that teachers should 'model competent speech and show [students] the difference between clarity and slang'.[20] But the imprecision, confusion and lack of genuine language awareness here make this an entirely incoherent instruction. Can slang not be a part of competent speech? And why is slang necessarily lacking in clarity? Do they actually mean slang, or do they perhaps mean colloquialisms or items of regional dialect? It is impossible to make out.

And then, of course, pupils themselves might not acknowledge the validity or authority of their teacher's variety of speech. One teacher told us about some experiences in their own school on the south coast of England, with a predominantly well-to-do, middle-class intake of pupils:

> A Level Literature students have been known to mock the accents of their teachers at my school. For instance, a former colleague was visibly upset

when students mimicked her [working-class, regional] accent, even though she was the only faculty member with a PhD in English Literature. More recently, two colleagues from [a nearby industrial city] have been mocked by students, too. Another colleague, when training, spent some time at an exclusive boys' school in west London. She was affectionately regarded as an Eliza Doolittle type, even though it was her doing the teaching. She was from [an outer London borough] and has an 'Estuary' accent.

You can well imagine that the woman training at the exclusive boys' school probably didn't feel that she was being regarded as 'affectionately' as all that.

Now, you could discipline those boys, and the other children referred to here who mocked teachers for their accents. But to what end? Would it actually do anything to change their attitudes, or to shore up the teachers' authority? Like the question of slang and dialect usage which we looked at in Chapter 1 (with the 'Banned Words' notice and the 'Zero Tolerance' approach), this is surely an issue which is crying out for a measured, thought-through, language awareness approach. In this way, children would actually discuss and begin to understand the relationship between dialect and accent and between correctness and standardness, the social and historical origins of standard languages and prestige accents, linguistic prejudice, prejudice against regional and working-class accents, and all the rest of it. We will continue to argue throughout this book that classrooms are the most natural site imaginable for thinking and talking about these matters; for as we suggested in Chapter 1, schools can take an institutional decision as to whether people's language – that of both students *and* teachers – is to be viewed as a potential problem, or as a pedagogic resource. Where an integrated, language-aware approach is taken, perceived language problems can turn into learning opportunities.

Which brings us back, naturally enough, to the classroom scenario with which we started this chapter.

2.5 'Read it properly!'

So let's return to that classroom. A primary school TA is listening to a child read. The child produces a glottal stop for the word *bottle*, so that it sounds like 'bo'el' (/ˈbɒʔəl/). The TA says (kindly enough): *'Read it properly!'* – but was this the right response? In order to answer that question, you need to be very clear about what the purpose of the 'reading aloud' activity actually is. And the first thing to remember is that you are not teaching the child to speak – she already speaks her language. Reading a written text out loud is not the same as *speaking*. Second thing: you are not teaching her to speak RP (or if you are, then you need to consider why, exactly, you are doing this – and explain it to the child). In our example, the child recognised the same consonant as an RP speaker would, and produced it in a different, but equally valid way. That is, she recognised and read the word correctly, and produced the sound in line with the norms of the local area.

In having a child read out loud, then, you are teaching about the rules of writing/spelling in English. They are not the same as the rules for speaking in English, and the aim of writing is not to replicate spoken language – unless you're actually writing speech, of course, as a novelist might do. When a child learns to read, one of the things they have to learn (and are in fact learning through the reading aloud activity) is that there is not a regular one-to-one correspondence between sound and symbol in English. For example, all English speakers have to go through the process of learning that *through*, *enough* and *bough* all share the same sets of letters in the same order, but are pronounced quite differently.

If you were a teacher in France, meanwhile, teaching a French child how to read, you might come across:

> *Elle voudrait* 'she would like'
> *Elles voudraient* 'they would like'

Now, these two items are, of course, pronounced exactly the same in French. The meaning – that is to say, whether it is singular or plural, one person or more than one – will be clear from the context. In reading the words aloud, the French child is learning that when French is written, it includes letters that are not sounded when we speak. There's nothing particularly strange or even very difficult about this – it's just one of the things that French-speaking children have to learn about reading and writing their language. In the same way, if the child was an English RP speaker, would you say to her 'say it properly!' because she didn't pronounce the final /r/ sound in *butter*? No – because in that accent, the /r/ is silent, while in many American and West Country accents, say, the /r/ would be sounded (the feature that linguists call *rhoticity*). Would you force a child from Sheffield or Newcastle to say *bath* with a long /a:/ sound? No, because in the child's natural accent the /a/ is a short vowel.

In linguistics, to put it in technical terms, we would say that the short /a/ and the long /a:/ in *bath* are just two different *realisations* of the same written vowel. Both are equally valid, and which one you use depends essentially on where you were brought up. Therefore, if the child pronounces *bottle* with a glottal stop (like this – /ˈbɒʔəl/), the adult really should accept the child's pronunciation! When the TA 'corrected' the child and told her to 'say it properly', she was confusing speaking and writing. The child is learning the rules of how English spelling corresponds (or not) to the way she speaks. The primary aim of writing in English is not to replicate exactly the sounds of spoken language. Reading out loud is not the same as speaking. A reading class is not a speaking class.

From a language awareness perspective, a reading aloud activity is perhaps best thought of as an opportunity for learning about speaking and writing, and how those things differ. You could illustrate this with videos of different people reading the same (Standard English) text but in their different accents, because different speakers will realise letters and words in different ways. Interestingly, an extreme example of this disconnect between writing and speaking occurs in the Chinese family of languages (which Chinese people tend to think of as varieties of the same language, but which are really different languages which happen to share the same script). A speaker of Mandarin and a speaker of Cantonese will read the same text, but produce entirely different words and sounds. They cannot understand each other's spoken languages, but they can both read the same characters and get the same meaning from them.

So to say 'read it properly' is to suggest that the way the child naturally says it is not proper, or not good enough. As recently as the 1960s it was far from uncommon for left-handed school children to have their left hand tied behind their backs, in order to force them to use the 'correct' hand for writing, because it was regarded as somehow abnormal to be left-handed. Indeed, we are just old enough to have a friend who actually had this experience. Think then, how the child feels if they are told that they don't speak properly, that their natural way of speaking has to be corrected, no matter how awkward this might feel. To quote M. A. K. Halliday again, from some sixty years ago:

> A speaker who is made ashamed of his [sic] own language habits suffers a basic injury as a human being: to make anyone, especially a child, feel so ashamed is as indefensible as to make him feel ashamed of the colour of his skin.[21]

2.6 Conclusion

As we noted at the beginning, sadly, few linguistics graduates enter teaching. Many teachers have very limited basic linguistic knowledge, and even teachers of English and MFL can qualify to teach without having any knowledge of linguistics. So it can be difficult to have conversations about even some of the basics of language. For example, that standardness is not the same as correctness – it's a pretty fundamental principle of linguistics that if a community of native speakers are saying a thing and they're saying it systematically, then it's not a mistake. Or that it is unhelpful to ban students' natural speech, or to 'correct' it in an unfocused way: so when Standard English is taught, it should be taught with the awareness that register and appropriacy are paramount, and that speech and writing will vary according to context. Or, of course, that speech is not just writing said out loud – it has its own rules and conventions.

In this chapter we have tried to illustrate how a lack of language awareness among teachers and policy makers impacts on approaches to language at school. Next, we turn to the question of the so-called 'language deficit' or 'language gap', and discuss the responsibility that all teachers have to develop the language skills of their pupils.

Notes

1 Cushing, I. (2021), 'Policy mechanisms of the standard language ideology in England's education system'. *Journal of Language, Identity & Education*. DOI: 10.1080/15348458. 2021.1877542

2 Cushing, I. (2019), 'The policy and policing of language in schools'. *Language in Society* 49: 425–450.

3 https://assets.publishing.service.gov.uk/government/uploads/system/uploads/attachment_data/file/244216/English_Glossary.pdf

4 https://www.theschoolrun.com/what-is-standard-english [Accessed 12/08/2021].

5 *Dialect* in linguistics is usually defined along the lines of 'a systematically differing, rule-governed variety of a language'. It has no connotations of good or bad, right or wrong.

6 Hogg, R. and Denison, D. (2006), *A History of the English Language*. Cambridge: CUP, p. 285.

7 Cushing, I. (2020), '"Say it like the Queen": the standard language ideology and language policy making in English primary schools'. *Language, Culture and Curriculum*. DOI: 10.1080/07908318.2020.1840578

8 At this point it would be helpful to everyone if we were to insert a snappy, authoritative, one-sentence definition of what Standard English is. Unfortunately, there isn't really one. That's part of the problem, and that's why it's so important that children learn about language and how it works, rather than just being told 'Speak correctly!'

9 English, F. & Marr, T. (2015), *Why Do Linguistics?* London & New York: Bloomsbury, p. 237.

10 https://www.dixonstc.com/why/oracy [accessed 12/08/2021].

11 Carter, R., Hughes, R. & McCarthy, M. (2000), *Exploring Grammar in Context*. Cambridge: CUP, p. 486.

12 Biber, D. & Leech, G. (1999), *Longman Grammar of Spoken and Written English*. Harlow: Longman, p. 50.

13 Halliday, M. A. K. (2004), *An Introduction to Functional Grammar* (3rd edition). London: Routledge, p. 8.

14 On page 94 of the 1769 Dublin edition, to be precise.

15 https://www.tes.com/news/why-i-insist-standard-english-my-classroom

16 See e.g. Wolfram, W. & Schilling, N. (2016), *American English: Dialects and Variation* (3rd edition). Hoboken, NJ: Wiley-Blackwell.

17 Cushing, I. (2019), 'The policy and policing of language in schools'. *Language in Society* 49: 425–450.

18 These are transcriptions made using the International Phonetic Alphabet or IPA (see Glossary).

19 Donnelly, M., Baratta, A. & Gamsu, S. (2019), 'A sociolinguistic perspective on accent and social mobility in the teaching profession'. *Sociological Research Online* 24 (2). DOI: 10.1177/1360780418816335, p. 3.

20 Cushing, I. (2020), '"Say it like the Queen": the standard language ideology and language policy making in English primary schools'. *Language, Culture and Curriculum*. DOI: 10.1080/07908318.2020.1840578

21 Halliday, M. A. K., McIntosh, A. & Strevens, P. (1964), *The Linguistic Sciences and Language Teaching*. London: Longman, p. 105.

3 Why every teacher is a language teacher

3.1 Introduction

It's hardly controversial these days to suggest that improving students' language skills must be the responsibility of every teacher, and in this regard at least we are wholly in agreement with the whole-school approach to language taken by successive governments via their DfE campaigns. However (and it is a big 'however'!), we do not think that this is best achieved by imposing blanket policies about Standard English or 'speaking in full sentences', or – as we shall see in a moment – by applying quick-fix solutions. The path to rounded language development lies through genuinely language-aware teaching. That is to say, language work needs to be carried out within the context of a whole-school language awareness policy, with language awareness embedded in every area of the curriculum, and with training and support in language issues offered to all teachers as a matter of course. We will make the case here; then later on we'll talk about how to 'design in' language awareness in all subjects (in Chapter 4), and how to organise school-wide resources to develop language policy and practice (in Chapter 8). We will also note in passing that many English teachers, because of their academic background and training, are rather ill prepared to push back against 'quick-fix' policies; we discuss the question of English teachers' roles and responsibilities in Chapter 5.

To begin this chapter we look at the idea of 'cultural capital' and the supposed language gap or deficit, which together form the background to the current intense focus on 'correct' language use – a focus which perpetuates the idea of language as being essentially a matter of right and wrong. We illustrate how it has led to the largely misunderstood emphasis on such things as 'Standard English only' and 'complete sentences' that we discussed in Chapter 2. And while we will begin by accepting, in part, that there may be issues regarding some children's communicative skills, as successive governments have suggested, at the same time we want to be absolutely clear. 'Deficit' is not the most helpful term, *and* the supposed deficits are often not really deficits at all, *and* this discourse unfairly favours the speech of middle-class children while marginalising the speech of others. What's more,

DOI: 10.4324/9781003201281-4

the solutions currently favoured by government and some academy trusts, like the imposition of speech codes or the decontextualised memorisation of vocabulary banks (see Chapter 4), are unlikely to resolve the problem, because they are not rooted in sound linguistic principles.

3.2 Language as 'cultural capital'

In 2013, the then Education Secretary Michael Gove used a term first coined by the Marxist theorist Pierre Bourdieu when he said: 'The accumulation of cultural capital – the acquisition of knowledge – is the key to social mobility.' Gove used this concept because, he explained, he wanted to enable disadvantaged pupils to have the same opportunities in life as their more middle-class peers, who often took their cultural experiences for granted. Ofsted picked up on the term – perhaps with some government encouragement? – and subsequently used it in its Inspection Handbook. It still had a prominent position in its guidance documents in 2019, when schools were being required to 'adopt or construct a curriculum that is ambitious and designed to give learners, particularly the most disadvantaged, the knowledge and cultural capital they need to succeed in life'.[1]

So when Ofsted inspectors visit a school, they are officially looking for evidence that it is furnishing its pupils with enough of this cultural capital to get on in life. Now, there isn't much wrong with this as a concept: it is surely part of a school's duty to equip a young person with what they need to benefit from and become a contributor to society. One aspect of cultural capital is what Bourdieu referred to as 'embodied' cultural capital. A good chunk of this, according to the theory, resides in how you speak – so children should learn to speak competently. Again, nothing wrong with that. But where there *is* a problem is in how the government and some schools view students' speech, in what they think 'good' or 'competent' speech is, and in what they are doing to show that the supposed deficit in cultural capital is being rectified.

Take as an example one particular school in north London,[2] which, like many belonging to academy trusts, has embraced the mantras expounded by the US educationist Doug Lemov in his *Teach Like a Champion* programme. Lemov's approach insists that students use 'standardised English' at all times and speak in 'full sentences' (the faulty foundations of which we explored in the previous chapter). In this school, in addition, just to make sure the students don't drop into bad habits brought in from home, they are not allowed to speak to each other in the corridors. When they are allowed to speak to their peers, they are forbidden from using any 'slang' – though that is never properly defined, or differentiated from colloquial or dialectal use of language.

We should point out immediately that the way these rules are framed suggests strongly where they originated. This is a discourse borrowed in large part from the context of heavily ghettoised American cities, where the variety of English known as AAVE (African-American Vernacular English) or 'Black English' might be a child's dominant or even sole medium of communication, and where other models of English are only intermittently present.[3] It is not at all obvious that this approach to dealing with language (even if we were to accept that it is a valid one in itself) can simply be picked up and dropped into British cities and schools, in the way that commentators of varying political persuasions are rather wont to do; the social, historical and linguistic environment is radically different. Certainly, there are characteristically 'black' styles of speech in the UK, with influences from e.g. Jamaican patois and west African languages, but such varieties as Multicultural London English (MLE) typically draw from a wider pool of influences (including e.g. South Asian languages and working-class 'cockney'), and tend to be used by a serially overlapping and racially disparate population of speakers.

However, even if we leave this to one side, while the expressed intention behind all of these rules may be to equip disadvantaged pupils with much-needed cultural capital, from a language education point of view there are aspects of the whole project which sound alarm bells. First, it assumes and establishes that any kind of spoken expression that is not Standard English is to be considered not just less valuable than the standard, but actually unacceptable as communication. Your two choices are Standard English, and silence. Most tellingly, 'speaking correctly' is listed as one of the school's *behaviour* policies, so that to speak using local dialect forms or with slangy street expressions is to break school rules – putting it on a par with smoking, swearing or chewing in class. 'Good' spoken English and good behaviour are apparently two kinds of the same thing. If this rings a bell to you, it's probably because this kind of discourse has been around for generations. Here are two examples which have become so famous (or infamous) that they have actually made it into the A level English Language syllabus as texts for discussion, thus achieving a kind of bizarre immortality in classrooms all over the land.[4] Back in 1985 the then Home Secretary Norman Tebbit said:

> If you allow standards to slip to the stage where good English is no better than bad English… these things tend to cause people to have no standards at all, and once you lose standards then there is no imperative to stay out of crime.

And more recently, following widespread riots in England in 2011, historian David Starkey mused on 'a particular sort of violent, destructive, nihilistic gangster culture' which had supposedly become fashionable. This culture revealed itself in language use:

> [B]lack and white, boy and girl, operate in this language together… This language which is wholly false, which is this Jamaican patois that has been intruded in England and that is why so many of us have this sense of, literally, a foreign country.

What is so striking here, as many newly language-aware A level students have, of course, noticed for themselves, is the way both Tebbit and Starkey associate non-standard language not just with deficit – not even just with wrongness – but actually with *criminality*. In the case of Tebbit, speech is perceived as somehow a moral issue, a matter primarily of maintaining standards of behaviour, rather than a matter of choosing the words most appropriate to the context. In the case of Starkey, the widespread and essentially unremarkable youth sociolect known to linguists as MLE, which we referred to above, and whose influences do indeed include Jamaican and other Caribbean voices, is racially pathologised and qualified as an 'intruder'. In rather the same way, some academies seem to suspect that the wrong kind of English will lead inevitably to wrong-doing. And inevitably, those children who haven't grasped that they should be using Standard English by the time they are in primary school are deemed to be part of a societal problem.

In this kind of discourse, then, giving children access to much-needed cultural capital is not quite what it appears to be, or pretends to be. It is less a case of widening their horizons than of trying quite deliberately to cut them off from their linguistic and cultural roots, marking their natural speech (as natural as a private school pupil's Standard English with an RP accent, remember!) as deviant and even obscurely dangerous behaviour. We saw in the last chapter that this attitude to standard and non-standard language has no basis at all in linguistics; it surely can't have much pedagogical validity, either.

3.3 Gaps and deficits

The question of cultural capital, and of what to do if children are perceived to be deficient in it, arises before those children have even commenced formal education. Successive governments have tried with varying degrees of success to tackle what has been called the 'last taboo' of education: what children learn from the age of 0 to 3, while they are still at home. We're going to explore this later on in the chapter, but for now, let's recognise that children do not start on a level playing field on their first day in Reception. However, the fact that a child cannot communicate in a way expected of him or her when they start school does not mean that they cannot communicate.

A colleague of Steve's once recounted how in a south London primary school where she used to work, children from a middle-class background started school more confident in certain skills than some working-class children. This included the learned behaviour of holding a book. They couldn't necessarily *read* much of the book – sometimes, in fact, they held it upside down – but they knew how to handle one, because they had seen books being used in their homes. Some home environments reflect and anticipate the middle-class norms of the school, and some do not. This is also true of language. As Steve's colleague went on to emphasise, while the less privileged children generally arrived in the school environment with little knowledge of Standard English, they were just as able as the middle-class children to communicate orally with their peers and teachers: some more so.

This is something that would be familiar to Basil Bernstein, the British sociologist and educational linguist whose name still routinely makes an appearance in BEd and PGCE courses because of his influential, controversial and often-misunderstood work in the 1960s and early 1970s. Having noted that otherwise academically able working-class school children tended to fare badly in language-based subjects, Bernstein investigated how children from working-class families used language rather differently to their middle-class peers. He categorised the different styles of speech used by the two groups as 'codes'. The working-class children used a 'restricted' code; for example, they assumed that listeners shared their own understanding of the topics discussed, and so used fewer complex sentences and a less extensive vocabulary. However, middle-class children, while they also used the restricted code in appropriate circumstances, were able *in addition* to use the 'elaborated' code when the situation demanded it. In this style of speech, they did not assume that listeners shared their understanding of topics, so would use more explicit language, and would not expect listeners routinely to infer meanings from the immediate context.

Now, you might conclude, and many people – including government ministers – appear to have done so, that what Bernstein was saying was that middle-class language is good (that is, sophisticated), while working-class language is bad (because it is unsophisticated). He wasn't saying this, though. With hindsight, he should probably have chosen a better word than 'restricted', or at least a word less open to misunderstanding. But like any linguist, he was describing what he observed, not making a value judgement on it. Nevertheless, Bernstein's formulations probably helped fuel the already current perception that there existed a 'deficit' or 'gap' in the language of disadvantaged children, and that it was the duty of schools to address it.

This perception has never gone away. Nearly half a century after Bernstein's early work, in 2018 the then Education Secretary declared:

> It is a persistent scandal that we have children starting school not able to communicate in full sentences, not able to read simple words. This matters, because when you're behind from the start you rarely catch up. Your peers don't wait, the gap just widens. This has a huge impact on social mobility.

He was referring to a study carried out by the DfE which suggested that 28 per cent of four- and five year-olds didn't have the communication skills expected of them. But there's a problem here. This politician was conflating two quite different aspects of language, suggesting that they are the same kind of thing. He was doubtless right that most children starting school should be able to read simple words. But what about children being unable to 'communicate in full sentences'? Does he perhaps mean 'speak' in full sentences? But as we have seen, *nobody* naturally speaks in full sentences – sentences belong to the realm of writing, not speech, so he is confusing two quite different forms of communication. Let us be clear: we do not claim that there is no problem, and we do think that disadvantaged children should be targeted for extra help and support. Indeed, one very substantial recent survey by researchers at UCL Institute of Education suggests that the key determiner of children's vocabulary skills at the age of 14 is the vocabulary skills of their parents, and that there is a *big* difference between the vocabularies of children with more and less well-educated parents.[5] However, the way these concerns are routinely aired in the political sphere is so obviously lacking in precision and language knowledge that it is very difficult to accept them at face value or, indeed, take them seriously. One must therefore wonder if what that politician really means is that working-class children don't use the 'elaborated' code characteristic of middle-class speech. If that is the case, then the problem he identifies is not really one of children not being able to communicate properly. Rather, it is that there is a disconnect between the sociolinguistic environment of the home and that of the school, with the result that they might not be communicating in a way which is valued by the wider society in which they are expected to thrive. To put it another way: most children, provided that they have the expected cognitive abilities for their age, are capable of communicating: but not always in a way that conforms to higher-status norms, and certainly not always in Standard English. A serious approach to this issue demands clarity and precision about what is actually under discussion here.

Plenty of professional educationists and linguists are sceptical about the whole notion of a 'language gap'. One at least has called it simply 'a myth'; so if ministers want it to be taken seriously, you might well think that they need to do rather better than this. Regardless, this is the background against which the DfE has launched repeated campaigns to address the supposed deficit. In 2019 for example, it announced a series of initiatives to halve the number of children starting school with 'inadequate speaking and reading skills' by 2028. One of these initiatives involved private companies like Clarks, W H Smith, Lego and Greggs 'playing a bigger role in children's education' (see Section 3.4 below). And, of course, back in school, and especially in the larger academy chains, a popular solution to fix the deficit and close the gap is to impose the strict requirement that from the time that a child is in primary school he or she should be using Standard English. But as we showed in some detail in the last chapter, this is not as simple or uncontroversial as it sounds.

The National Curriculum is dotted with references to Standard English. Ofsted insists upon it; some academies insist it is spoken at all times; Standard English is referred to in the English Language GCSE Mark Scheme. As English specialists, we come across the term Spoken Standard English when we assess KS4 students for their Spoken Language Endorsement, a qualification awarded by the examining boards but separate from the English GCSEs, although delivered by English departments. The mark scheme for this qualification defines Spoken Standard English like this:

> For the purposes of the spoken language assessment, use of Spoken Standard English means that a learner must –
>
> - be audible,
>
> - be intelligible, and
>
> - generally use language appropriate to the formal setting of the presentation.

This is really a very eccentric definition of 'standard'. What on earth has being audible got to do with it, for example, or even being intelligible? These are obviously to do with *how* you speak, rather than the form of the grammar and vocabulary that you use. None of this encourages any confidence in the supposed experts' grasp of how language works.

The debate about making Standard English the default code for schools is obviously not a new one, but it has only been since the introduction of academies in 2008, and especially the widespread streamlining of the National Curriculum in 2013, that many schools have felt the need to impose a vision of what they think Standard English is and why everyone should speak it. Interestingly, some schools are interpreting the increased vagueness of what Dan Clayton calls 'the stripped down version' of the National Curriculum to impose much more prescriptive rules about what Standard English is and how it should be taught, to the exclusion of all other varieties and dialects.

For some radical or 'critical' linguists, to mandate Standard English is to 'locate the problem within the speaker', in the words of a 2022 article by Ian Cushing and Julia Snell,[6] and especially so when the speakers concerned are from minority ethnic backgrounds. They insist that from a 'raciolinguistic perspective', the children should not feel that they have to modify their language in any way: it is up to the school and the wider (white) society to learn to hear them properly and to accept that their way of speaking is appropriate. In their historical analysis of documents produced in the 1980s by HMI (the predecessor of Ofsted), Cushing and Snell argue that, in requiring children to learn how to modify their accents in order to be understood outside their own speech community, HMI was actually contradicting its own advice that children's home speech should not be 'criticised, belittled or proscribed'. And they see a direct line from that 1980s advice to the approach taken by the present-day Ofsted, where for example

> [a] 2018 report of a Bradford school with a community of primarily Pakistani and Roma students from low-income backgrounds was praised for how "adults teach children to speak in standard English" and "speak clearly and encourage children to repeat what they say".

Note that this, for these authors, is far from being a positive thing.

We do not entirely share this view of the situation. Certainly, in an ideal world everyone's natural speech would be judged acceptable and appropriate at all times, by everyone else. This is because, as we emphasised in Chapter 2, for linguists it is axiomatic that non-standard language is as good, whole and proper as the socially privileged variety which we call 'standard' language. But we don't live in an ideal world, and speakers make social judgments about other people's speech all the time. (And note, those doing the judging include working-class and minority speakers – it is not a one-way process!) To encourage children to believe that they should be able to always and anywhere speak just as they like, and blame 'society' for any negative consequences that might flow from this, risks coming across as either naïve or cynical. This applies even more obviously where the children do not have English as their mother tongue, as must surely be the case for a good proportion of these Pakistani and Roma children in Bradford. It is doubtless true that they face other obstacles in life, and that the acquisition of Standard English alone is unlikely to catapult them into the professional middle classes (the 'meritocratic myth', as this article calls it). On the other hand, however, will their life chances be improved if they simply fail to develop the skill of adapting their speech to the social context and prevailing social norms, as most speakers do? It seems unlikely.

Cushing and Snell in fact state their political position very plainly: 'For us, social justice is only possible through the dismantling of structures and the redistribution of power, rather than the model of linguistic assimilation which underpins the inspectorate's approach.' For what it's worth, we would argue that developing the skill of code-switching between registers is hardly 'linguistic assimilation'. More importantly, though: to insist that society should be made to adapt to speakers, rather than speakers to society, is possibly a defensible ideological position to hold, but it is not a practical one, and it does nothing at all to help working-class and minority children in the here and now. It sometimes feels, oddly, that these authors are taking a parallel approach to the adherents of Doug Lemov – though from a very different political perspective – and overlaying ethnolinguistic models developed in the urban United States onto the very different reality of the UK. As we remarked in Section 3.2 above, we don't really have an equivalent to AAVE. By the same token, most linguistic discourses in the UK are not particularly racialised (the MLE, all-race *innit*, for example, tends to be just as stigmatised as the predominantly black-identified *bare*, and disapproval of such terms is usually mainly class-based), while to talk of Ofsted having 'white ears' has to us an oddly transatlantic ring.

The problem, in reality, is not that Standard English is being taught, or even that it is being positioned as a model. It is that it is too often being taught in an uncritical and non-language-aware way. It is too often being taught by teachers who don't really understand what Standard English is, and believe it to be simply 'correct' or 'proper' English. We would advocate critical, language-aware teaching of the standard, where children are encouraged to actually discuss, analyse and understand what Standard English is and how it came about, and compare it with the other ways in which they speak and write. So while we don't agree entirely with the more radical position, we can see how the lack of language awareness and the clumsiness of government policy invite this kind of political reaction. For example, as academy trusts and Teach First have increasingly embraced the linguistic principles of the *Teach Like A Champion* programme, there have been recurring attempts to 'ban slang', as we saw in Chapter 1.

This kind of thing takes us about as far away from properly informed language policy as it is possible to get. No attempt here to encourage students to think about register (that is, the way language varies according to context). No informed comparison of one style of speaking with another. No thought given to how speech and writing differ, or how different types of speech and writing are typically organised. No attempt to discuss or define what 'slang' actually is, or differentiate it from colloquialisms or dialect usages. In short, no language awareness at all – just straightforward diktat. What we have here, then, is one more example of language rules being laid down by people who don't understand how language works, and perhaps don't really *want* to understand, because it goes against their assumptions and prejudices about how different people talk.

And there's more.

3.4 Multitasking sales staff and non-interfering teachers

In 2019 the British government announced that it was going to tackle what it called, as we saw in the previous section, the 'last taboo in education' – children's early language development in the home environment. It did this by calling on the help of 'author ambassadors', publishers and retail outlets in a quest to improve disadvantaged children's literacy and communication skills. This 'national mission' received the support of W H Smith, Clarks Shoes, Lego, Arriva and Greggs, among other familiar names. There were to be book giveaways and learning apps and the like; but most eye-catching was the plan to train volunteer staff from these companies to develop 'speech, language and communication development'. Some 6500 Clarks staff were to be asked to 'engage children in conversation to improve language skills, and help build their confidence in social situations', while Arriva would 'begin training frontline staff with early education tips to help engage with children using their trains all over the country'.[7]

Now, this was not of course quite the full story, and in any case, as far as we can discover, this initiative never really quite got off the ground – but it gives us a small indication of how the government was thinking about society, language and communication. For a start, did they really think that the most socially and economically deprived families bought their footwear from the solidly middle-class Clarks, or routinely whizzed around on the UK's notoriously expensive trains? This misapprehension apart, it is notable that the onus to improve children's language was not placed on linguists, or even teachers, but on sales staff who were supposed to… do what? Teach children new vocabulary while measuring their feet or scanning their train tickets? Now, that's multitasking!

It's possible (if you try quite hard) to see how conversation with adults in service encounters might be of some benefit to some linguistically deprived children. But how does that fit with the focus on 'correct', i.e. Standard English? Or is it the case that the training purportedly to be given to shop and train staff would actually include an acknowledgement that Standard English is *not* always appropriate or necessary? In which case, why is this not thought to be a useful principle for school teachers, too? Well, the clue is here: 'The government pointed to analysis from the National Literacy Trust suggesting 7.1 million adults in the UK have very poor literacy skills' – and here: 'W H Smith will advise parents in Swindon, which has relatively high levels of illiteracy, on how to support their children's language development'. That National Literacy Trust research was in fact very heavily criticised when it came out, and it is hard to see why W H Smith employees should be experts in language development, but that's neither here nor there. The point is that the campaign is being driven by concerns about *literacy* – speaking is being mixed up with writing, as if they were just two ways of representing the same thing.

So we return to a well-worn discourse. Non-standard speech is equated with lack of communication skills and poor language development, and poor literacy is equated with not speaking properly. The conviction that there is a direct link between 'speaking properly' and writing Standard English, of course, has been around for a long time. It came up notably in 2010 when the then Mayor of London, Boris Johnson, commissioned a Centre for Policy Studies report on literacy and language skills among London schoolchildren, entitled *So Why Can't They Read?*[8] Tellingly, the person entrusted with this was Miriam Gross – a distinguished literary editor, to be sure, but not a linguist or educationalist.

In the report, she duly makes the usual connection between low literacy attainment and speaking 'street', by which she simply appears to mean MLE: 'This language contains a mix of various ethnic influences – Caribbean, Cockney, Afro-American, Indian and others…' She follows this up with the familiar point that teachers should help children distinguish between 'street' and the written standard. Primary school teachers, she says,

> encourage children to read poems and stories written in ethnic dialects – in Barbadian patois, for example – which is fine, but they omit to point out that there are linguistic discrepancies. Only later, when they get to secondary school, do these pupils discover that 'street' is not acceptable in their written work.

The throwaway 'which is fine', emitted through palpably gritted teeth, suggests that she at least half-accepts that non-standard language (including the odd-sounding 'ethnic dialects') can be included in classrooms alongside standard language.

But she doesn't follow this to its logical conclusion – that 'pointing out the discrepancies', or rather, as language specialists would say, the systematic comparison of different registers of language, should in fact form the very basis of an informed, linguistically aware approach to language work. Instead, she reverts to our old friend 'banning slang', supposedly because 'child-centred' teachers cannot be trusted with such a language-aware approach:

> In other European countries argot and slang are not allowed into the classroom; children know exactly what is 'correct' usage in their main language, and what is not.

This huge generalisation is debatable, to say the least, but let's stick with it for now:

> In this country, by contrast, primary school teachers – dedicated as many of them are to 'child-led' education – don't feel that it's their role to interfere with self-expression in any shape or form.

It is not at all clear, of course, that most or even many primary school teachers subscribe to this approach to children's language. But even if they did, this would hardly be an argument for banning home and street English from the classroom, in the way that she claims teachers in other countries do. Rather, it would be an argument for inclusive, comparative and linguistically informed teaching of literacy and oracy.

The Clarks Shoes project and the Gross report essentially amount to the same thing. It's a bundle of heavily ideologised policy, barely informed by the facts, and built as much on misunderstanding and class prejudice as it is on genuine engagement with children's language. But that's par for the course when policy is set by people with strong opinions about language but little language awareness or expertise. So who will rescue us – English teachers, perhaps? The problem is, though, that English teachers don't always know quite as much about language as the rest of a school thinks they do – we'll talk more about this in Chapter 5.

3.5 Every teacher a language teacher, every classroom a language classroom

Linguists sometimes talk about situations of 'diglossia'. This term refers to a situation common in bilingual societies where one language or dialect (known as the H or High variety) is associated with official contexts, power and prestige, and the other (the L or Low) with the home, the playground, the marketplace and so on. In such situations, one of the foremost objectives of schooling is to teach children to competently manage the dominant or official language of their country, so that they are able to take a full part in society and have a chance at making a success of higher education. Few people would disagree that Moroccan or Iraqi Arabic speakers should learn Modern Standard Arabic, for example, or that Swiss German children should also learn Standard German, or that Jamaican schools should teach Standard English to children who speak *patois* at home. But as sociolinguists have consistently argued, the so-called 'High' variety should be taught intelligently and sensitively, in a linguistically informed fashion – it is neither kind nor productive to attempt to ban, marginalise or belittle the students' natural way of speaking.

The UK as a whole is far from being diglossic these days, although it is worth remembering that England at least was in just this situation for some centuries after 1066, when the ruling classes spoke Norman French and most other people spoke English. This is why we still have that divide in English between 'high-flown', formal words derived from Latin through Norman French, and 'ordinary' Germanic-English ones – think *recline/lie, construct/build, precipitation/rain* – that sort of thing. However, the language education principle applies in much the same way. As far as we are concerned, the question is hence not whether children should learn to communicate in Standard English, but *how* they learn to do so, and what they also learn in the process about how language works. So we certainly do not disagree that Standard English should be taught. Nor do we disagree that, as successive governments have argued, children need focused language work in order to develop an ability to communicate appropriately in context. The problem, as we have already argued, is that when management teams try to deal with the issue by mandating language 'solutions' across the curriculum and throughout the school, these solutions tend to be superficial and linguistically uninformed. Making every teacher a language teacher cannot mean imposing Standard English across the board, banning slang and fillers, forbidding talking in the corridors, insisting on children speaking in complete sentences or demanding that pupils learn banks of vocabulary at a rate of 300 or 400 terms a year (something we discuss in the next chapter).[9]

A school built on language awareness principles would instead require every teacher to be able to model excellent communication skills and to show children how to negotiate the different uses of different Englishes: standard and non-standard, high register and low register, depending on the context, purpose and audience. That is to say, what the child learns should be the vital life skill of being able to communicate in the appropriate register for the context in which they find themselves. Rather than insisting on language enforcement in the school, we would like to make a case for classrooms to be seen as sites of language *noticing*: a natural forum for ongoing exploration, discussion and debate about language.[10] While English and MFL classrooms would seem to be particularly natural spaces for this kind of work – assuming the teachers concerned are comfortable with it, and are prepared to own the identity of 'language specialist', which we discuss in Chapter 8 – all classrooms should be sites of linguistically aware teaching. We will get into the more specific *how* of this in the next chapter.

As a first step towards the linguistically aware classroom, school leaders might wish to consider avoiding talk of gaps and deficits. We would argue, in line with

Bernstein, that there very rarely exists a 'deficit' as such (though it's true that the children of more educated parents tend to have larger vocabularies, as we saw in 3.3 above). What there definitely is, is difference – and it is this difference, or rather the kaleidoscope of differences, which makes language study so interesting and rewarding. Children are already fairly adept at recognising different styles of speech and writing. They code-switch all the time, although, of course, they will need some structured help in discerning when it is appropriate to speak in one way or another. Just like the rest of us, they have to negotiate the different kinds of language they encounter daily, regardless of class, background, age or ethnicity; children's language knowledge is therefore a resource to be explored and exploited in teaching, not an alien presence that must be kept out. Even children who arrive at school with little or no knowledge of English do not arrive with no knowledge of *language*. Teachers should therefore consider avoiding talking of 'correctness'

Justin Bieber and the primary school prescriptivist

The policy-driven insistence on supposed 'correctness' (i.e. standardness) in all contexts has given rise to some fantastic social media sideshows. Twitter and Facebook are reliably full of examples of questions from the KS2 SPaG test in which the choice of correct answer is arguable or simply unknowable, and of teachers and parents poking fun at them. Meanwhile, in 2016 a primary school teacher went viral with a Facebook post of a letter one of her pupils had apparently written to Justin Bieber.[11] The pupil took issue with Bieber's song 'If I was your boyfriend' and upbraided him for his incorrect use of grammar:

> In the song you can be heard – on a number of occasions – stating 'If I was your boyfriend'. Here you have clearly used the subjunctive mood incorrectly. The correct lyrics should in fact be 'if I were your boyfriend'.

Having established the nature of the error, the pupil waved aside any potential objections in advance: 'You may reply to this by stating that such grammar inaccuracies are not of any importance. I strongly disagree.' She or he then went on to admonish Bieber for his lapse:

> As an Upper Key Stage Two pupil, currently studying hard for my Punctuation and Grammar test, I find it incredibly disappointing that you are unable to follow what is [sic] considered to be the basics of the English language.

The newspapers had fun with this, of course, and it was presented as an entertaining story: it was a 'grammar beat down', said the *International Business Times*, while *Metro* commented 'Yikes. Well, that's Justin told.' But it's not really as entertaining as all that, when you stop to think about it. From a functional point of view, the grammar of the lyrics is *not* incorrect: the line is surely couched in a register suitable for its purpose and audience. It's a disposable pop song, written in the voice of a teenager, not a legal document or a speech in the House of Lords. If Bieber, or the song's narrator, had used the highly formal (some might argue archaic) *if I were*, wouldn't the girl thus addressed have thought him nerdy or, worse, 'lame'?

The pupil – guided, we can only presume, by the teacher – has learned little about context or appropriacy. They have learned a certain *form* of Standard English, but seem to have learned nothing about its *functions* – about what standard language actually does, and why we express things as we do. Falling into line, the *IB Times* called Bieber's grammar 'sloppy' – which is an interesting echo of non-standard language being equated with moral decay or poor behaviour. Such are the pitfalls of a blind imposition of Standard English in the classroom. It is certainly not wrong to teach children to recognise the need for, and be able to confidently handle, standard usage in context. But it *is* wrong to teach children that Standard English is appropriate in all situations. It's the job of the teacher to help the child recognise when to use Standard English, and just as important, when not to. Otherwise, we don't produce linguistically sensitive, careful communicators – we produce pedants.

when it comes to speech, and think instead in terms of appropriacy to context, the way linguists do.

Non-standard speech does not poison the well. As we suggested in our discussion of the Miriam Gross report in Section 3.4 above, teachers should be systematically working with it, not working against it, banning, ignoring or marginalising it. It is not our intention here to criticise teachers. Indeed, they are to be praised sincerely for their dedication and creativity; but they do need to ensure that their efforts are focused on what works and what lasts. And, of course, English teachers have a particular responsibility here. In an online review of a memoir entitled *Let That Be A Lesson*, written by a former English teacher, the reviewer noted the following:

> There are the (again) routine attacks on the government's not unreasonable desire for pupils to have a secure understanding of English grammar. In my experience, it is only English teachers who find this so outrageous, believing that rules inhibit creativity and freedom of expression. Imagine a music teacher arguing about whether to teach scales and arpeggios.[12]

Hmm. All right, it's mischievous – but it's not, perhaps, entirely mistaken. Some teachers are very resistant indeed to the idea of teaching grammar, at least in the way that successive governments have required them to do (and we talk about this in detail in Chapter 5). Conversely, there are teachers who become so lost in the nuts and bolts of grammar that they forget that the point of this grammar is to enable the speaker or writer to *do* things with language.

Take the experience related in the *London Review of Books* by one concerned parent (an academic, though not in the field of language), with 'guided reading'. Before the Covid-19 pandemic, he tells us, he had been unfamiliar with this phenomenon. Now, though, with schools being closed he found himself in the position of having to help his eight-year-old daughter manage it. She was 'sometimes required to read the same short passage five days in a row and to perform different tasks in relation to it', he explains, 'presumably... for her to learn how specific sentence constructions work, in the hope that she would be able to apply that knowledge elsewhere'. However, to his dismay, the focus remained on mechanical manipulation of sentence constructions, and 'the invitation to write autonomously, beyond a sentence or two, never arrived'. He remarks:

> It wasn't merely the emphasis on obscure grammatical concepts that worried me, but the treatment of language in wholly syntactical terms, with the aim of distinguishing correct from incorrect usage.

Well, quite. And he goes on to make a very apt comparison:

> This is the way a computer treats language, as a set of symbols that generates commands to be executed, and which succeeds or fails in that task.[13]

English teachers should really not be in the business of resisting the very idea of explicit teaching about grammar. Nor should they be, though, in the business of drilling children in grammar to such an extent that there is no room for creativity and self-expression. An awareness of grammar, and, most importantly, how to teach it in a constructive and contextualised way, is part of the package, just like awareness of how standard languages came about, how speech differs from writing, when slang and fillers are appropriate, and all the rest of it. If we are to escape the numbing effect of things like guided reading, clumsy constraints on students' speech and snake-oil miracle cures for linguistic 'gaps', then English teachers, especially, need to be – or be willing to become – *language* teachers in the fullest sense.

3.6 Conclusion

Geoff Barton has written that 'knowing about vocabulary is the responsibility of every teacher'. We would concur: however, we would go further and say that having an informed knowledge of how language works is the responsibility of every teacher, and the entitlement of every child. This includes not just standardness, and not just words and grammar, but also the way discourse is structured, for example.

A colleague once asked whether he, as a geography teacher, should point out a pupil's overuse of filler words such as 'like' when they're speaking in class. The answer, of course, is that it's all about appropriacy to context (in language, almost *everything* is about appropriacy to context!). If the pupil is answering a question, and so thinking on their feet, as it were, or making a casual reference to something, then no – why would you? But if the pupil is making a formal, prepared presentation on the Ice Age or oxbow lakes or something, and the use of *like* is distracting and interferes with their main point, then our answer would be yes. Helping students get their ideas across effectively is part of the deal, whatever your subject, as two teachers who talked to us about their classroom language work explicitly pointed out:

> What is structured talking? If you mean, do I prepare students to make spoken presentations, then – yes. They are given ideas about how to structure a verbal presentation, often depending on the topic. Openings and closings are referenced. Often, persuasive devices are referenced.
>
> (Katy, English)

> Pupils have to give developed answers to questions which we start by preparing this style of learning from year 7.
>
> (Ruth, MFL)

Teachers, inescapably, need to consider language, in its fullest sense, as being at the heart of their professional expertise. Not just Standard English, then, or subject-specific vocabulary; and for English teachers, not just literature, or the ability to spot a subjunctive, but how language works in context (and see the Justin Bieber Text Box!). Of course, there has long been a campaign to promote literacy across the curriculum, a recognition that it is not just the job of the English teachers of a school to address reading and writing. While this is to be applauded and encouraged, there needs also to be a concerted focus on language across the curriculum, and in the form of a whole-school policy. This is not just about reading: it is about language awareness and using language appropriately. As a starting point, this should certainly include ensuring that teachers, whatever their speciality, should never feel that good teaching or the following of government mandates requires them to make children feel embarrassed or inadequate because of how they speak.

Having argued here that all classrooms can potentially be viewed as sites of language work and language awareness, in the next chapter we move beyond policy and turn our attention to the 'how to'. That is, we look at the actual practice of language awareness at school, considering how language work can be embedded in all the different areas of the curriculum and how, exactly, teachers can work systematically on developing student language awareness.

Notes

1 https://www.gov.uk/government/publications/education-inspection-framework-overview-of-research

2 For a detailed discussion, see Cushing, I. (2021), 'Language, discipline and Teaching Like a Champion'. *British Educational Research Journal* 47 (1): 23–41.

3 See Alim, H. & Smitherman, G. (2012), *Articulate While Black: Obama, Language, and Race in the US*. Oxford: Oxford University Press, p. 191.

4 Clayton, D., Goddard, A., Kemp, B. & Titjen, F. (2015), *AQA English Language: AS and A Level*. Oxford: OUP, pp. 171–172.

5 Sullivan, A., Moulton, V. & Fitzsimons, E. (2021), 'The intergenerational transmission of language skill'. *British Journal of Sociology* 72 (2): 207–232.

6 Cushing, I. & Snell, J. (2022), 'The (white) ears of Ofsted: a raciolinguistic perspective on the listening practices of the schools inspectorate'. *Language in Society*. DOI:10.1017/S0047404522000094

7 https://www.gov.uk/government/news/society-wide-mission-to-tackle-early-literacy-and-communication. It was reported widely at the time; for example in *The Guardian* and *Retail Gazette*, both 30 January 2019.

8 https://www.bl.uk/collection-items/so-why-cant-they-read

9 And if you *are* going to focus on teaching vocabulary, it needs to be done in a properly contextualised way, as Alex Quigley suggests in his book *Closing the Vocabulary Gap* (Routledge, 2018).

10 Tim has written about this in detail elsewhere – see Chapter 13 of English, F. & Marr, T. (2015), *Why Do Linguistics?* London: Bloomsbury.

11 See for example the report in *Metro*, 9 March 2016.

12 https://thecritic.co.uk/beating-a-dead-narrative/

13 William Davies, *London Review of Books*, 24 February 2022, p. 5.

4 What language awareness looks like

4.1 Introduction: doing (the right) stuff with (the right) words

Early in the new year – a busy time for sixth form tutors as their charges finish their personal statements for their UCAS applications before the January final deadline – a colleague from a different department emailed me (Steve):

> *Sent: 18 January 2022 08:28*
>
> *To: CollinsS*
>
> *Subject: question about a word?*
>
> *Hi Steve*
>
> *Is the use of 'ameliorate' correct for a student's personal statement?*
>
> *'My completion of the Bronze Duke of Edinburgh award, and my ongoing involvement in Silver, has allowed me to ameliorate my map reading skills and my ability to work in a team.'*
>
> *Hilary*

Clearly, the student had got the wrong word here – but you can see how. They'd presumably been looking for a synonym for 'improved', googled for an alternative, and been presented with this option. And while 'ameliorate' does indeed mean to make better, it has the very specific meaning of making better in the sense of mitigating something bad or making it more tolerable. It tends to be found alongside (or as linguists would say, it collocates with) words like *problems*, *conditions*, *suffering* – not with map reading.

Over lunch we mentioned this to a teacher friend, who reminded us of the joys to be had in learning lessons from TV comedy. He pointed us to an old episode of *Friends*, in which the reliably dim Joey Tribbiani has been asked to write a recommendation letter to an adoption agency to help Chandler and Monica adopt a child. Joey decides to try to sound 'smart' and impressive by using a thesaurus – for every

DOI: 10.4324/9781003201281-5

word. He proudly tells Chandler how he managed to improve his original phrase about them being 'warm, nice people with big hearts' by rendering it as 'humid, prepossessing homo sapiens with full-sized aortic pumps', adding solemnly: 'And hey, I really mean it, dude'.

Joey is, of course, advised by his friends to not try to sound smart but just to be himself. Wise words. All too often, students get the impression that by using long, complicated words they will automatically achieve good marks – but that isn't how it works. Psychologist Adam Galinsky of Columbia University even talks about the 'Complexity Trap', by which he means that sometimes when people use complicated language they can actually tend to 'come across as low-status or less intelligent [...] Complicated language and jargon offer writers the *illusion* of sophistication, but jargon can send a signal to some readers that the writer is dense or overcompensating.' To mention Bernstein one last time, it can feel as if someone who is aware that they are functioning with a 'restricted' code is trying hard to develop an 'elaborated' one, but mistaking what the key characteristics of that code are. If you remember our brief explanation of diglossia in English in Section 3.5 of the last chapter, you will recognise that what is happening here is that our writers are replacing mainly shorter, Germanic words with mainly longer, Latinate words in the belief that they are 'posher' and therefore automatically more high-status and impressive.

So certainly words are important and yes, it's great to widen one's vocabulary. The currently popular idea of the 'word gap', which we discuss more fully in a moment, is an effort to respond to this perceived need. But in the way that we suggested earlier, from a linguistics point of view words are only useful in their functional context: in their relationship with other words, in how they create meaning, or add meaning to something. As Andrew McCallum of the English and Media Centre (EMC) says: 'Words cannot be treated simply as items of knowledge to be entered into the memory banks of pupils, because their meaning depends upon the particular context in which they are used.' Essentially, where both Joey and our sixth-former have gone wrong is not in not having enough words (anyone can hit the thesaurus!) but in failing to match their words appropriately to the surrounding context. Frontloading words can only go so far, because you can't make words work for you in isolation: you need to use them in conjunction with other words in order to make phrases; to make a sentence; to make paragraphs; to create discourse in order to produce a particular communicative outcome. To put it another way, if we really want to see children use language effectively, whether in science or geography, poetry or maths, then we need to teach them how to think in a rounded way about what linguists call register – that is, how to choose the most appropriate language for the context, the communicative purpose and the particular social setting.

In this chapter, and building on the foundations laid out in Chapter 3, we offer some suggestions as to how this can be achieved by making language visible in the classroom through the encouragement of active language noticing tasks. We will develop the idea of working with different written genres used in different subjects to demonstrate the importance of thinking beyond the level of just 'words' to the level of discourse – coherent stretches of language used for a meaningful communicative purpose. What underlies this approach is our belief that the single most effective way in which a teacher can help a child who has only had access to the 'restricted' code (however we choose to understand that contested term) is to give them an awareness of higher, more formal and academic registers of language along with the confidence to use them.

We noted in the last chapter that there is some resistance to this and we acknowledge that not everyone agrees with this way of seeing things. According to the 'critical' view, it is society and schools who should adapt the way they perceive and use language, not children themselves. However, as we also noted, the likely practical outcome of this approach is that children might fail to acquire the forms of language that the society around them values most. Those who argue that working-class children should not be obliged to master 'higher' forms of language are invariably themselves highly educated professionals, usually university academics, with an impressive grasp of Standard English and academic register: should not these prized resources be available to all, now, in the society that we all have to live in?

That said, we do actually agree with quite a lot of what the critics of the 'Standard English ideology' have to say. Like them, and in contrast to the *Teach Like A Champion* ethos, we believe strongly that there is nothing wrong with the way that working-class and minority ethnic children express themselves; but we think that they also need to acquire other ways of expressing themselves. When schools try to achieve this in the clumsy ways we discussed in our earlier chapters (e.g. 'Banned Words'), we don't really think that this is principally down to racism, elitism or classism (though there might well be elements present of all three) – it is mainly down to lack of understanding about language, and specifically, about what standard language actually is. In short, we are arguing for language awareness and for linguistically sensitive approaches to teaching about language in the society in which we live now, rather than the society which we might wish to see in the future.

In that spirit, let's take a closer look at the idea of the so-called 'word gap'.

4.2 *Is the gap really a word gap?*

A country clergyman told me that he believed the labourers in his parish had not 300 words in their vocabulary, and a recent article in the Quarterly extends the statements to the great mass of our rural population.

Alexander D'Orsey, Professor of Public Reading at King's College London, 1864–1890[1]

Obviously, different people have differing sizes of vocabulary, and certainly the more education people have, the more words they pick up. However, one thorough research study suggests that an average school leaver probably has a vocabulary of 10,000 or so words, while some others have claimed that the total might be twice that.[2] It is just not conceivable that a healthy adult could have a lexicon limited to 300 words, or even 3000 for that matter – even an uneducated rural labourer in the nineteenth century. So it is much more likely that what we have here is a combination of class prejudice and misplaced diagnosis, and that what really shocked and disappointed the clergyman was the distance between his flock's language and the registers and vocabulary of educated, Standard English that he would regard as 'proper'. It might be that the overlap between his and their vocabulary was quite limited: would he know local, rural words like *yaffle* and *snotgogs*?[3] Whatever, the important thing to note for our purposes is that rather than commenting that the labourers perhaps had a rough and ready way of expressing themselves, or used non-standard words, the clergyman framed the problem as a shortage of vocabulary.

Is it perhaps possible that people are *still* doing that?

We spoke in the last chapter about the concept of the 'language gap' and the resulting government-led push to have Standard English taught universally. From the early 2000s on, much work in this area developed a very specific focus on vocabulary. There was a flurry of research and publicity about a supposed 'word gap', as academics, politicians and media commentators perceived a specific need to increase the actual number of words which underprivileged children had at their disposal. The OUP's Oxford Language Report, which we cite below, is one example of the kind of publication which has been widely circulated – the website accompanying its 2021–2022 update invites schools to 'Join Us As A Word Gap Partner School' and 'commit to closing the word gap'.[4] And as with the 'language gap' in general, there was also a certain amount of push-back against the whole idea, with critics suggesting that the supposed gap was a myth or that this was just another way of marginalising and denigrating non-standard speech.

We don't intend to get caught up in these debates, though for the record we are happy to accept in principle that a 'word gap' might well exist. It is substantiated by the researchers from UCL Institute of Education whom we referred to in Section 3.3 of the last chapter; and most teachers, of course, are aware of something like it. But our real point here is that language is about a great deal more than just words in the sense of lists of vocabulary in tiers of complexity (the 'tiered language' model that has become an increasingly popular tool in schools for thinking about vocabulary). It's about ways of expressing yourself; it's about selecting the appropriate communicative resources for the communicative effect that you wish to achieve. It's about how vocabulary meshes with and helps create genre (different kinds of written and spoken text) and register (the appropriacy of language to context). So we need to look at ways of working with an awareness of genre and register in all subject classrooms.

And in any case, sticking at the level of words: as Andrew McCallum has further pointed out on the EMC's blog,[5] subject-specific and specialist vocabulary, the 'key linguistic and literary terminology' that is specified for the National Curriculum and GCSE, is probably *not* actually the most important thing for the classroom teacher to concentrate on (it can often be learned fairly quickly and easily - even mechanically). What is more important is 'the language that, as a proficient adult reader, it is all too easy to take for granted' – that is, the more ordinary words, often with a range of subtly different meanings in different contexts, which occur with very high frequency in academic environments. McCallum gives examples such as *interpret/interpretation*, *represent/representation* and *illustrate/illustration*. The meanings of these words cannot simply be memorised from a list: they have to be understood through use in multiple contexts.

Later, we discuss how it's important that students have a variety of choices when expressing themselves, but let's stay with the idea of a word gap for a moment. Geoff Barton writes in the beginning of the Oxford Language Report *Why Closing The Word Gap Matters*:

> Thus the Year 10 pupil who says, 'At the start of the play Macbeth is a hero but at the end he is a villain,' will be judged as less intelligent than the one who writes, 'Although he begins the play a hero, Macbeth ends as a villain'.

Well, that's certainly a possibility. He then goes on: 'Yet this isn't a matter of intelligence. It's about vocabulary'. But there's a problem here. He's right that this is not a matter of intelligence – but the issue here is not one of lack of vocabulary. It's a question of sentence structure and discourse arrangement. It's a question of academic or formal *register*. Most children (not all) will know what 'although' means – it is not the same as not knowing what 'mycoplasmas' or 'serendipity' means. You probably don't need to have it explained to you by an older or wiser person; you probably don't need to look it up in the dictionary on your phone. You pick the sense of it up when you are learning how to speak and listening to others speak, even if you never actively use the construction yourself. So it's not the same kind of lack of knowledge as not knowing a specialist term. It's Tier 1, in the terminology of tiered language, or perhaps Tier 2 at a stretch.[6] But rather like that nineteenth century clergyman, Barton frames not knowing how to use 'although' as essentially a matter of limited *vocabulary*, rather than a lack of breadth in 'ways of writing' or 'ways of expressing yourself'.

Barton goes on to acknowledge this in part when he talks about teachers teaching the specialist language of their subjects – and students do, of course, need to be taught the terminology (words that are either unfamiliar or have specialised meanings, like *tectonic*, or *hegemony*, or *metaphor*). That goes without saying. But to use a subordinate clause which begins with the conjunction *although* is to show an awareness of how sentence structure helps create a scholarly style of expression. It's not just about vocabulary, it's about knowing how to recognise and use relevant genres and appropriate register, and how to structure an argument effectively. Sentence structure does things! Beginning a sentence with *although*, to continue with that example, is often used to signal that you acknowledge an opposing viewpoint, but are about to foreground a response to it. So *although* is not just a unit of vocabulary to be learned by rote. It is embedded into ways of arranging your phrases, ways of expressing yourself, and this can first be practised and refined in spoken English: in conversations in the classroom, as suggested in the EMC blog we mentioned just now.

It is quite probable that this is what the teacher we mentioned in Chapter 2 was groping towards – the one who wrote in the TES that he prepared his students to write by first making them speak in complete sentences. He was mistaken in thinking that 'speaking in complete sentences' is a thing, linguistically speaking. He was, though, absolutely right to sense that his students needed exposure to and practice with a register of English that was unfamiliar to them. The exposure and practice, then, are crucial. If you simply stockpile words and deploy them without really understanding the importance of context, then Professor Galinsky's Complexity Trap snaps shut: you risk sounding like a parody, or an uneducated person's idea of what a 'clever' person sounds like. In common parlance, you'll sound like you've swallowed a dictionary (or plugged yourself into an online thesaurus, like the sixth-former mentioned at the start of the chapter). You'll sound like Joey from *Friends*. Compare this with our story about Justin Bieber in the text box in Chapter 3: the kind of teaching that only focuses on one aspect of language risks producing not language-aware students, but pedants.

Here's an example of misfiring on register from the classroom. I (Steve) am asking my Year 9s who are studying *Great Expectations* to give me one adjective each to describe the main characters. One boy describes Miss Havisham as 'salty'. This is contemporary slang for 'bitter' - but it's an inappropriate word here because it's too informal, too colloquial. Now, if I'd set a comparative language awareness task of getting the children to describe the characters in the register of street or playground talk, then it absolutely would be the right word. The child understands exactly what Miss Havisham is like (she's salty, all right!). But he's preparing to write a formal essay, so 'salty' just won't do. He's not wrong, but he needs to learn to adjust his register.

As one teacher (and a highly language-aware one) put it to us, when dealing with a child's use of an inappropriate word it can be productive and enriching to treat this as a language-noticing and discussion opportunity:

> If it is a colloquialism I explain that that is okay and we explore different registers and what might cause offence or be less appropriate in a formal setting, etc. I emphasise that it is not 'wrong' as they are native speakers - but context is everything.
>
> (Susie, Latin and MFL)

Yes, indeed: as we noted previously, in language, it's *always* about context!

Of course, the 'word gap' diagnosis might be the right one: maybe the child just doesn't have a more appropriate word than 'salty' in his lexicon. But given time to reflect, he (or one of his peers) might well be able to come up with a more appropriate word, and in any case we potentially have a teachable moment, a learning about language activity. So there absolutely is a place for low register/home/street speech in the school. Ways of expressing yourself should be open for comparison, discussion, study and debate, and of course that is exactly what happens in language-aware classrooms. How else are children to understand how language works in different social settings? You understand language by debating and discussing it, working with it and experimenting with it, not by banning or stigmatising certain manifestations of it, as we argued in Chapter 2.

Clearly, linguists and the public don't always see eye to eye on this, as this tweet (which we referred to in the opening chapter), suggests:

> It's not just spelling & grammar. It's the way people talk too. That whole 'yes bruv innit'. Street talk. Give me a break. I was in primary school in the 80s. We had it drilled into us how to write, spell, grammar and pronunciation. Schools teach via tech now and miss the basics.

An academic linguist saw this tweet and responded to it with: 'Hi! Linguist here. Language change is natural and systematic. People use language to convey aspects of their identity. Kids also know how to "style-shift" without explicit instruction'. And he went on to suggest that this was basically all a lot of fuss about nothing. But is that *really* the case? Always? Certainly, most children do develop an awareness over time of when to style-shift or code-switch, adapt the register of their speech, but do they really always know all the more formal words, the academic discourse, without explicit instruction? Do they always know instinctively which words fit a particular context? The boy who said Miss Havisham was 'salty' clearly didn't. Sometimes teachers have to teach! Ray, a teacher of science, put it very simply and clearly indeed when we asked him how he dealt with children who struggled with the idea of adapting their language to the classroom:

> I explain that I talk differently in different circumstances and with different people.

Quite. So children do need new words, but they also need a broader awareness of appropriate register, which includes vocabulary but is not restricted to vocabulary. Look at the AQA A Level Biology 'key words' slides produced by the TES for free download.[7] These are excellent for the revision of key specialist terms – *ultracentrifugation, graticule, hydrolysis* and so on – but as the title 'key words' suggests, they are focused only on discrete terms. They give no indication at all of how these terms fit into the wider written or spoken discourses of biology. They don't tell us anything about other identifiable elements of general scientific academic register (e.g. multiple adjectives plus headword, sustained use of the passive voice or embedded clauses in complex sentences) or, crucially, about the typical features of texts in the specific field of biology. They are not presented as an element of the characteristic genres and discourses associated with biology – descriptions of processes, commentaries on labelled diagrams, lab reports, that kind of thing. Crucially, no examples are given of the words being used *in context*. The key words really are just key words. It's rather like the bit in *Hamlet* where Polonius enquires 'What do you read, my lord?' only to receive from Hamlet the deliberately unhelpful reply: 'Words, words, words'. Without a wider context, there isn't much meaning to be made.

Language awareness is not just about words, then, or tiered language. It's about grammar, genre, audience, tone, purpose and register, it's about how the whole of language works. The language challenge for subject teachers is to teach register and discourse as well as the technical and specialist terms of the subject. Universities commonly run courses in English for Academic Purposes or EAP (mainly for non-native speakers of English, but now increasingly for native speakers, too), and some of the approaches that they have developed can help us here, especially when they focus on discipline-specific language. Academic writing specialists like Ken Hyland and Fiona English have been arguing against EAP 'academic word lists' for decades now, on the grounds that they result in a mechanical style of writing and treat 'academic writing' as a single style or genre in itself – which it is not, as there are very many different ways of writing academically or formally, and they differ from subject to subject. We show an example of this kind of unnu-anced 'academic writing' advice at Figure 4.2 in Section 4.3.3, where we discuss it further. Katherine Mortimore emphasises the importance of subject specificity in her useful book *Disciplinary Literacy and Explicit Vocabulary Teaching*[8] – though we would argue that it is not only vocabulary that needs to be taught in this way. Writing (and formal speaking) is about so much more than words – not just choice of vocabulary, but choice of grammatical structure, textual organisation, what is foregrounded and backgrounded, the 'fit' between genre and register.

Genre and regenring

I (Steve) was helping my son with his history homework. After watching a number of clips on YouTube of Hollywood westerns, he had to compare how these movies rep-resented Native Americans and their historical reality. This was a fun task. We watched a John Wayne clip, a Looney Tunes cartoon and Johnny Depp in *The Lone Ranger*. The written task was fun, too – writing a letter to Sam Peckinpah explaining he had got the depictions of the Sioux all wrong and then persuading him to reshoot a movie, showing the truth. Now, what struck me, as an English teacher, was that here was a history lesson which was clearly combining the skills of understanding a historical topic, but also using language skills to demonstrate that understanding. In Fiona English's book *Student Writing and Genre* she proposes that students be encouraged to, for example, re-cast a formal essay on economics into the form of a radio interview. This is the type of task that pupils could be doing at an earlier age. It might be an activity at KS2, we may toy with it at KS3; but as children get older, the demands of examinations get greater, we are by that time ensconced in our subject silos, and none of us really thinks very far beyond the walls of our own subject classroom.

How might a regenring approach work? Well, for example, in a geography lesson, after learning about tectonic plates, students could:

- write the script to a section in an earthquake disaster movie

- imagine how a scientist explains an earthquake to her husband who doesn't know anything about the science

- record a TikTok of how two children might talk about it in 'street' fashion in the playground

Now, many busy teachers will retort: 'I haven't got time to teach it (regenring) because it's not in the exam.' Fair enough, but we would argue that you should teach this because it will actually make your pupils perform better in the exam – because they will be better attuned to the idea of genre, more sensitive to the uses to which language can be put, more skilled at making linguistic choices in order to fulfil different communicative needs. Genre rewriting and re-casting might also just be the sort of task to engage recalcitrant boys: those bright boys who enjoy science but find it hard to get ideas down on paper might relish the challenge of changing a text from one form to another.

So we don't just have a word gap, for the simple reason that we're not working only at the level of words. We have genres – the 'types' of text associated with a subject. And we have academic register, the formal style(s) of language that society tends to use to talk about academic subjects, and which children need to learn. And we have the broader concept of disciplinary discourse, the characteristic way of expressing things in a particular subject. So how do we set about working creatively and productively with the genres, registers and discourses of school subjects?

4.3 The language-aware classroom: working with genre, register and discourse across subjects

As you can probably tell by now, we believe that explicit language awareness teaching goes deeper than focusing on words and so-called 'tiered language'. Students and teachers need to know what words and grammar *do* in different contexts, and explicit language awareness teaching, which focuses on discourse, register and audience, does just that. In this section, we're going to look at some concrete examples of how to work with awareness of genre, register and discourse in different classrooms, and suggest that teachers can go beyond the concept of the 'word gap'.

4.3.1 It's all about context

I (Steve) often wonder how I can explain to school children that there really isn't that much difference between the Modern English we speak and the Early Modern

English used by Shakespeare. As soon as I start teaching Shakespeare, though, the children's response is that Shakespeare spoke Old English, with all those 'thee's and thou's'. I explain that although Old English is related to Modern English, it is very different in its grammar and much of its vocabulary. But Shakespeare's English is considered Early Modern and we can understand a lot more of it than we first think. The confusion they often feel is not caused by a lack of familiarity with the words themselves, but with how those words have been used. For example, I'm teaching a group of middle ability Year 10s. We're looking at Lady Macbeth's speech in Act 1, Scene 5, at the lines:

> *Art not without ambition, but without the illness*
> *Should attend it.*

They're struggling, but not because of the 'Art', an archaic rendering of the verb 'are' – I've explained that. It's not the vocabulary either. They certainly understand 'ambition', not least because we've already been exploring it as a theme central to the play. In fact, there are no words at all that they find difficult, but they still don't know what the lines mean. Is Lady Macbeth saying that her husband doesn't have an illness? What does 'attend' mean here? And how does that construction 'Without… should' work? What we have here is not so much a vocabulary gap as an example of how literary language, and especially highly imaginative language like Shakespeare's, operates. Ironically, some of this literary language tends to be the stuff that we remember 400 years later, the phrases that get used and mis-quoted and applied to daily life – 'Lead on, Macduff'; 'hoisted by his own petard'; 'Wherefore art thou, Romeo?' and that kind of thing – but a real engagement with the texts requires a reader to open themselves up to the possibility of new, unfamiliar meanings, or multiple shades of meaning, which is surely one of the reasons why we still teach Shakespeare in the first place. Some effort is needed on the reader's part, but there isn't a vocabulary gap as such.

You want to see a real vocabulary gap? Here you go:

> We will focus mainly on the Schrodinger equation to describe the evolution of a quantum-mechanical system. The statement that the evolution of a closed quantum system is unitary is however more general. It means that the state of a system at a later time t is given by $|\psi(t)\rangle = U(t)|\psi(0)\rangle$, where $U(t)$ is a unitary operator.

So far so obscure. But there's more:

> An operator is unitary if its adjoint $U^\dagger$ (obtained by taking the transpose and the complex conjugate of the operator, $U^\dagger = (U^*)T$) is equal $U{-1}$ to its inverse: $U^\dagger =$ or $UU^\dagger = 11$.

This is from a quantum mechanics textbook, and you will *only* be able to extract some meaning from this passage if you have studied a basic level of quantum physics and made the effort to learn some of the specialist vocabulary of that field. But note one important thing! Unlike the extract from Macbeth, the grammatical structure of this passage is actually very straightforward indeed ('We will focus mainly on...'; 'The statement is... more general'; 'It means that...').

So both these texts are tricky to understand, but not in the same way. It certainly can often be the case that the vocabulary of a piece of writing is obscure or difficult for students, and certainly the introduction of new vocabulary is an important part of a teacher's job. As we mentioned above, a big part of teaching a subject is to introduce its specialist terms. But the job of the teacher goes beyond that: not just to teach words, but to develop in the children an understanding of the characteristic discourse of that subject. Every teacher needs to develop in their students an awareness of how language works in the context of the subject.

A 2022 article[9] in the academic journal *Cognition* brings an interesting angle on this from the area of law, and specifically that of legal contracts. The authors analysed a corpus of 10 million words (with the help of a computer, we trust) and measured how difficult readers found it to understand the language of contracts compared to everyday written language like film subtitles and newspaper articles. Most importantly, they tried to establish *why*, exactly, they found it difficult. They concluded that while there might be certain archaic and rare words that people often have trouble with (like *hereinafter* and *to wit*), it is 'poor writing, not specialized concepts' that makes legalese difficult for most people to understand. Writers of contracts were prone to, for example, over-using the passive form for no good reason ('The right to trial is waived by the parties'); throwing in distractingly random capitals ('ALL WARRANTIES ARE HEREBY DISCLAIMED'); and, worst of all, embedding clauses in the centre of other clauses:

> In the event that any payment or benefit by the Company (all such payments and benefits, including the payments and benefits under Section 3(a) hereof, being hereinafter referred to as the 'Total Payments'), would be subject to excise tax, then the cash severance payments shall be reduced.

Structures like this, the authors pointed out, have been shown repeatedly by linguists and cognitive scientists to be 'notoriously difficult to process'. So again, we see that what looks on the surface like a word gap might not really be a word gap at all. Legal contracts could be much more easily understandable, while remaining legally watertight, if the people who wrote them were more concerned with the experience of the reader. Good writers, like good readers, concentrate on bringing out meaning, of which the actual meaning of individual words is only one part. Children need help to begin to develop this awareness of different meanings, by seeing through demonstration how discourses differ depending on context and register.

4.3.2 Narrowing the discourse and register gap

There are already a number of excellent resources available to help make the shift from thinking at the level of words to thinking at the levels of discourse and register: Debra Myhill has created the LEAD Principles, for example, which focus on using real texts and stress the importance of discussion when exploring language choices.[10] This goes beyond the idea of tiered language. Rather, it provides suggestions for teaching metalanguage (that is, the language used to describe language, which we return to in Chapter 5) and explicitly teaching how texts are put together for specific purposes. It even pairs skills: writing like a scientist and writing like a poet; using subordinate clauses with non-finite verbs to provide layers of detail in a history text. Andrea Macrae's stylistics-focused teaching, meanwhile, explores how looking at patterns in language is a useful way of understanding how language works in different contexts.[11] Focusing on the patterns in a text, and importantly, when those patterns are broken, will lead to discussion about how language can be used for communicative effect.

In the English classroom, Marcello Giovanelli and Dan Clayton have reminded teachers how profitable it can be to discuss in a classroom context the numerous attempts by some academies to ban 'slang'[12] (remember our discussion in Chapters 1 and 2). These lessons can be enhanced by analysing leader comments and opinion pieces about current language usage, written by journalists from a prescriptive perspective. Students could then try writing a persuasive letter back to the newspaper arguing why slang should be allowed or discussed in the classroom context. The EMC's Language Laboratory[13] has a whole series of lesson plans which focus on creating a discursive debate about Standard English. Fiona English has explained the benefits of recasting a text in a number of different ways in order to explore different communicative effects on knowledge-making[14]; and in another book I (Steve) have explored how the teaching of a Sherlock Holmes story can be approached on a number of levels.[15]

When I do this, before discussing the richness of Conan Doyle's imagery and gothic tropes, I guide students towards focusing on sentence-level analysis, and particularly on analysing Holmes's utterances linguistically. What is the effect, for example, of his use of declaratives and imperatives? How does Conan Doyle use orders and statements in Holmes's utterances to give the impression that he is super-confident but also infuriatingly bossy? This sentence-level analysis could easily be adapted to other subjects. For example, what sort of sentence forms are needed to explain an experiment in biology? In a moment we will show some examples of how language-aware teachers in other disciplines can make language more visible in their humanities and science lessons. But first, as an English teacher myself, it seems sensible to start off with illustrating how I introduce explicit language awareness teaching into my own lessons.

I'll stay with Macbeth to illustrate how noticing language can provide an alternative way of approaching any text. The default position of most students, perhaps encouraged by their literary-minded teachers, will often be to look for imagery in Shakespeare. But what if, while we keep imagery at the back of our minds – we will return to it in this lesson – we focus for a moment on the *grammar* – the machinery, the nuts and bolts of how Shakespeare organises his text? Here is what I mean. Let's look at a GCSE question, based on Act 1 Scene 5 of the play, which includes Lady Macbeth's famous soliloquy:

> *Glamis thou art, and Cawdor, and shalt be*
> *What thou art promised. Yet do I fear thy nature;*
> *It is too full o' th' milk of human kindness*
> *To catch the nearest way. Thou wouldst be great,*
> *Art not without ambition, but without*
> *The illness should attend it. What thou wouldst highly,*
> *That wouldst thou holily; wouldst not play false,*
> *And yet wouldst wrongly win. Thou'dst have, great Glamis,*
> *That which cries 'Thus thou must do,' if thou have it,*
> *And that which rather thou dost fear to do,*
> *Than wishest should be undone. Hie thee hither,*
> *That I may pour my spirits in thine ear*
> *And chastise with the valour of my tongue*
> *All that impedes thee from the golden round,*
> *Which fate and metaphysical aid doth seem*
> *To have thee crowned withal.*

In this typical AQA English Literature GCSE task,[16] students are first given some context, explaining that Lady Macbeth has just finished reading Macbeth's letter about his meeting with the three witches. Then comes an extract from the soliloquy, and the question which follows asks students to 'explore how Shakespeare presents ambition in this speech' and also 'in the play as a whole'.

Now, the extract contains one of Shakespeare's most famous phrases: 'too full o' th' milk of human kindness', as well as giving us the enduring image of Lady Macbeth using incantatory language, 'Hie thee hither', to draw Macbeth to Dunsinane. She is successful, as he arrives on stage moments later. What is often overlooked in approaching this text, though, is Shakespeare's use of modal auxiliary verbs ('wouldst', 'must', 'should'). I might ask the pupils, after reminding them about what types of verbs modals are, to write down the different verbs and the different effects they create. They will have learnt about modal auxiliary verbs at KS2 but may need to have their memories jogged, and it could be a good opportunity to go beyond the idea that verbs are merely 'doing words' and explore the functions of, say, primary, stative and active verbs. Lady Macbeth, addressing her husband although he is not in the room (yet!), almost spell-like, says what he *is* and what he *shall* be. Her declarative statement here demonstrates her certainty that the Weird Sisters' predictions will come true. For her though, there is a problem – he is not ruthless enough:

> *too full o' th' milk of human kindness*
> *To catch the nearest way*

She then uses a series of modal auxiliaries – *wouldst* appears six times in an extract of only sixteen lines. Such frequency must be worth thinking about. What does it mean, exactly? Why is Lady Macbeth stressing what her husband *would* like to have? How much does he want the crown? I will have explained how modal auxiliaries can be used to express varying degrees of possibility and prediction, or obligation, or permission. The modal auxiliary *should/shouldst* appears twice, first to show that he hasn't got the ruthlessness to be a murderer ('illness that should attend it'), then to express that he won't regret his actions ('should be undone'). The soliloquy ends with her commanding him to come to her: 'Hie thee hither.' The effect is instant. The spell is cast, and Macbeth walks on stage. So rather than solely focusing on the imagery here, a language-aware lesson can home in on grammar – the verbs, specifically – to suggest, perhaps, that Lady Macbeth's will is so strong that what she wants to happen, will happen. Grammar is creative – it is active in making meaning.

We will turn now to how we can promote language awareness in other subjects by looking at what happens linguistically in different subject areas. What we're proposing here is that teachers be encouraged to look at the language they use in their subjects using some of the insights and technical apparatus of linguistics; going beyond the simplistic 'word gap' model to see how language operates at various levels.

4.3.3 Using linguistics to incorporate language awareness into other subjects

One way to support fellow teachers across other disciplines is to help them in directing students towards the appropriate communicative resources for their subject. This can be done effectively by borrowing a concept from linguistics. English Language A Level students will be familiar with what are called language 'frameworks', 'levels' or even 'toolkits'. These frameworks are used to analyse how different features of a text are used to achieve a particular purpose for a particular audience. Students are expected to understand and use these 'levels' when undertaking AS and A Level English Language; both exam specifications make it a requirement to analyse a text linguistically, and these levels are a tool to help them focus on particular discrete areas.

The language levels go from bottom (the smallest units of language) to top (the largest), though you can arrange them the other way round if you prefer. On the bottom level of the framework we find phonetics – the production of individual speech sounds – and phonology, which is how these sounds work in the sound system of any given language. Moving up to the next level we find morphology, which deals with how words are formed, and syntax, the rules by which words combine to form strings of language like clauses, sentences and spoken utterances. Morphology and syntax are together referred to in linguistics as morphosyntax, which is what is known in everyday usage as 'grammar' – the structural rules by which words are created and combined in order to produce meaningful language. We then have lexis and semantics, which deal with vocabulary and meaning. And then there is pragmatics, a broad field which covers how language is used and understood in social context. At the very top of the levels is discourse, an even broader concept, which looks at how texts and genres are constituted. The examination boards add graphology to this list of levels, which relates to how language is represented by visual signs, and might include anything from a 'no entry' sign to hieroglyphics. The linguistics purists among us, of course, might narrow their eyes here and point out that writing is not language – it is a technology used to represent language, as we noted in Section 2.3 of Chapter 2.

The idea of borrowing these frameworks into other subjects is to help students to answer the questions: what is the text trying to achieve and how is it trying to achieve it? The levels could well be the actual focus of English language lessons, unlike a chemistry lesson where the focus is more likely to be atomic structure or something. But they can still act as an aid to teachers of other subjects by pointing their students towards the appropriate tools in the language toolkit for each subject. Writing up a science experiment will make much use of the passive voice ('Five 50-mL beakers were used to contain the water…The water was applied to microscope slides using 1-mL plastic pipettes'); history essays tend to require ample numbers of discourse markers and pronouns as cohesive devices, and so on. And if we are using the same terminology to describe language in all subjects, then children begin to notice the linguistic links between subjects, and eventually to become more broadly skilled writers, readers and speakers. There is, then, no reason why a chemistry or geography teacher should not be using in their classroom terms borrowed from linguistics, like morphology or discourse. They are simply tools to help students focus more effectively on how language is used.

If we look at a very helpful, discipline-specific poster in our history corridor (see Figure 4.1), we can see how a language-focused approach can help students understand what they are doing with language in their work in history. This is just the sort of way in which language-aware colleagues across the school can build a pupil's language awareness. The non-language specialist might need some help, however, not in delivering lessons on the appropriate grammar required for the relevant communicative resources (or to put it another way, the appropriate tools from the language toolkit), but in being able to recognise themselves what the

Figure 4.1 'How to improve your writing in History' corridor poster display.

language is *doing*. And English teachers need to lay the groundwork of language resources as part of their teaching, so that pupils can recognise them and use them in other lessons.

At the discourse level, this poster lays out pretty clearly how to write an essay – how to formulate arguments and counter-arguments as an aid to explaining how or why something happened and the importance of that event, by offering a selection of discourse markers under the *Supporting your claims* heading. At the grammatical level, there are a number of adjectives, adverbial phrases, different types of verbs (active verbs, some passive verbs and modal auxiliary verbs) used for different purposes, such as to *change pace* or *change extent*. In fact, observing some of the language features taught in a history lesson, I was struck by the clear links between what we do in English and what is taught in humanities, the only real difference being that language resources are taught less explicitly in the latter. This needn't be so. I'm not suggesting that non-language specialists should do the job of English teachers, but more coordination between departments, training in INSETs, and yes, reading this book(!), will mean that teachers, and eventually therefore pupils, will see more clearly the language links between each subject.

Staying in history for the moment, but linking back to the discussion on academic writing that we started in Section 4.2 above, some schools are now providing their subject area teams with academic writing style sheets like the one in Figure 4.2.

Academic Style

1 Use formal vocabulary.
✗ Influential kings and queens like...
✓ Influential monarchs such as...

2 Avoid two-word verbs
✗ Subsequently, the country was broken up into smaller states.
✓ Subsequently, the country was divided into smaller states.

3 Use the full forms of verbs.
✗ Henry VIII didn't have a male heir.
✓ Henry VIII did not have a male heir.

4 Use formal grammar structures (noun phrases and clauses). Avoid too many simple sentences.
✗ After the war, many people migrated. There were many reasons for this.
✓ After the war, there were two main reasons for migration.

5 Use statements. Avoid rhetorical questions.
✗ Why did peasants rebel against Richard II in 1381?
✓ Peasants rebelled against Richard II in 1381 because... .

6 Be as precise as possible. Use exact figures and values.
✗ The Industrial Revolution, which lasted for over 100 years...
✓ The Industrial Revolution, which began in 1750 and ended in 1900...

7 Use hedging (tentative language) such as *possibly, may, might, could*. Avoid absolute statements.
✗ The invention of the printing press is the most revolutionary development...
✓ The invention of the printing press might be the most revolutionary...

8 Use impersonal language (There is... It is.., passive voice, no adverbs showing your feelings).
✗ Sadly, Gavrilo Princip assassinated Archduke Franz Ferdinand.
✓ Archduke Franz Ferdinand was assassinated by Gavrilo Princip.

Adapted from www.eapfoundation.com

Figure 4.2 Academic style sheet for History (adapted from The EAP Foundation).

Now, while there might possibly be some scraps of good advice here, none of it is actually presented as advice. What we are given is a series of assertions, with mechanical 'right' and 'wrong' examples (notice the clumsy crosses and ticks), which are likely to produce a correspondingly mechanical response in children – avoiding rhetorical questions or simple sentences, for example, when these are in fact essential instruments in the language toolkit. And a fair amount of the advice is downright misleading, to put it as politely as possible. There is usually little wrong with using 'two-word verbs'; English, like its cousin German, is full of them and they can lend a helpfully punchy and earthy feel to a text when that is what's needed. So while teachers might want to suggest alternatives (in this case a Latinate verb such as 'divided'), it is simply not true to state that usage of a particular word type is 'wrong' per se: again, it's all about choosing the most appropriate words in order to achieve a particular communicative purpose. As we pointed out at the beginning of the chapter, a text composed of nothing but Latinate words is unlikely to sound 'clever' or formal: it's more likely to read like something written by Joey from *Friends*. And as for some of the other advice: well, why should one not use adverbs to indicate a particular position with regard to a statement? That is something of a mainstay of academic writing, as we note in Section 5.5 of the next chapter. And is it really always necessary to be as precise as possible? Surely too much precision can be as unhelpful as too little? Doesn't it *always* depend on the context, the type of text, the intended audience, and so on?

In short, this kind of style sheet is a very, very blunt instrument, which ignores context and in addition makes not the slightest accommodation towards the fact (which we noted in Section 4.2 above) that academic writing is always, to a greater or lesser degree, *subject-specific*. We would encourage a language-aware history department to adapt the style guide, or, better, write their own, offering alternatives and explaining what is going on in each example. They could provide more detailed definitions of what the different linguistic features are, using precise terminology for 'tentative language' (modal auxiliary verbs) and 'two-word verbs' (phrasal verbs), and encouraging students to use some types of adverbial phrases, such as 'clearly' and 'possibly' so that students begin to develop a sense of when to use different communicative features in different contexts. Meanwhile, up the corridor in the geography department, the language frameworks will look broadly similar, but also rather different. Unlike their historian colleagues, geographers might want to discourage students from using modal auxiliaries to register doubt and speculation when writing about phenomena in physical geography, but might encourage the use of tentative language when exploring effects of human geography: the causes and effects of global warming, for example.

4.3.4 Language awareness in science

What about a subject which is ostensibly not 'writing-heavy'? Communicating in biology, chemistry and physics relies just as much on choosing from the communicative resources, and the choices will be somewhat different, but they will also have things in common with more writing-based subjects. The excellent 'Read like a…' posters, produced by Jennifer Webb of Funky Pedagogy (see Figure 4.3), demonstrate the similarities that exist across communicative resources in different disciplines. Webb has developed a whole set of these discipline-specific learning

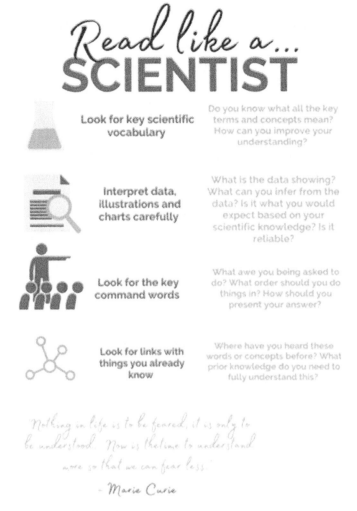

Figure 4.3 'Read Like A Scientist'.
Source: Funky Pedagogy

resources; they are focused on reading rather than writing – but it all contributes to raising language awareness, of course!

Dr Joanna Rhodes, a science teacher in Huddersfield, explains it like this:

> We teach [scientific terminology] with the assumption that students will pick it up as they go along. Addressing the language of science as a linguistic phenomenon, explaining how certain words are constructed, and helping students to understand and use these is crucial in helping them to understand and engage with aspects of the scientific method and to improve extended writing.

This is it exactly. What are the characteristic forms and patterns of language used in science subjects? Or, to put it another way, what would a language-aware approach to science teaching look like? Firstly, in science subjects, perhaps more than elsewhere, there is a consistent emphasis on precision measuring and accuracy, which is reflected in lexical precision: the noun 'volume' needs to be used instead of 'amount', when talking or writing about the quantity of liquid or gas a container can hold; 'weight' is not used as a measurement term in physics, where 'Newton' is the correct term for measuring how heavy an object is; and so on. There is thus often a tension or potential confusion between everyday language and subject-specific terminology, which teachers might draw particular attention to. Teachers are often adept at teaching key words, through a number of different strategies. They can teach terminology, for instance, by linking a root word to its etymology. This is the level that linguists refer to as morphology, where the individual building blocks of words are analysed, and so links can be made between words via their shared roots. My biology colleague explains the meaning of photosynthesis, for example, by inviting students to think about words like photograph and photocopying.

What science teachers need to do then is take the escalator up to the next level of language and explore the *discourse* of their subject with their students. What does a typical written answer look like? What are its grammatical features? It is by having this discussion that we can really improve literacy and language awareness by taking it out of the English classroom and into the rest of the school. So, if we turn to grammar in science we will find something just as productive as we did in history. Take chemistry, and look at this sample GCSE exam answer.[17] The question states: 'In the UK, potable (drinking) water is produced from different sources of fresh water. Explain how potable water is produced from fresh water.' 'Student A' answered as follows:

> Firstly we must find a fresh source of water, for example, surface water, surface rain, or groundwater. Then in order to remove any solids, for example, twigs the water must be passed through filter beds. Finally we sterilise the water to kill any microbes using either ozone, chlorine or ultraviolet light.

Now, the answer is a good one, well-formed and articulate, and deserves the good mark it received. The punctuation is not brilliant, but the grammar is sound and there is good use of sequential discourse markers ('Firstly'/'Then'/'Finally'). Arguably, though, the student would have been better served overall and in the long term if they had been taught to make systematic use of the passive voice, which is after all the characteristic form of describing and explaining processes in science and technology. Note how the form of the examiner's question invites this!

Explain how potable water **is produced** from fresh water.

A language-aware science teacher would be pointing out to students that the grammatical clue to how to go about writing their answer is in the question itself. So, an ideal answer might look like this, with systematic use of the passive voice:

Firstly, a fresh source of water is found, for example surface water, such as rain, or groundwater. Then, in order to remove any solids, for example, twigs, the water is passed through filter beds. Finally, the water is sterilised to kill any microbes, using either ozone, chlorine or ultraviolet light.

And so we help develop the student's awareness of discourse, that is to say, the characteristic patterns of language associated with a particular subject or context. The added value here lies in the fact that language awareness – awareness of discourse and register, as opposed to simply technical terminology or formal Standard English – helps students in any subject. They will understand what it means to 'explain' as opposed to 'plan' in the last example. This will help them in the future, whether they become biochemists, football commentators or marketing executives. Crucially, it will help them in the abrupt transition from GCSE to A Level, and the even more abrupt one (especially for working-class students) from school to university or further study.

Now let's look at a sample answer to a 6-mark biology GCSE question in which the student has been asked to 'plan an investigation' into the effects of light on seedling growth.[18] The student begins:

Firstly you take 3 boxes and then use the scissors on one box to cut holes in the lid, on another box cut holes in the side of the box then another box leave with no holes in. Then take three pots of seedlings and place one in each box.

While the language is a little uneven, it is already evident that the student knows what to do, linguistically speaking – whereas we, as non-scientists, initially looked at this question and had little idea how to approach answering it. When asked to 'plan an investigation' in biology, how do you start? With 'I would'? With 'we must'? Do you use bullet points? A numbered list, perhaps? Even with a PhD in linguistics, you can find yourself honestly at a bit of a loss, because this demands subject-specific, context-specific language knowledge. The student continues in the same confident manner:

After this use 3 lamps that are exactly the same therefore being in control, and use one lamp to shine on the box with the lid holes, one with the holes in the side of the box and one with the box that has no holes in. Then leave the seedlings to grow for seven days.

So from this answer, it is apparent that a language-aware teacher has explained the written form demanded by a 'plan an investigation'-type question – the student has used imperatives ('take', 'use', 'leave') and sequential discourse markers ('Firstly', 'Then', 'After this'). Language-aware teaching aims at giving the students the linguistic tools they need to recognise and negotiate the particular language characteristics of the subject and the task. That's the kind of teaching this student got.

One crucial element that they have evidently been taught is the concept of 'command' words. Ofqual, the exam regulator, requires all exam boards to use command words in all subjects to indicate what they are expecting the student to do in terms of function. (And if you look again at Figure 4.3, you'll see an explicit instruction to students to pay attention to these words.) However, knowing which particular grammatical structures are characteristically used to achieve a particular function is something that only comes through language-aware teaching: which grammatical structures and other linguistic features are typical of each task, in each discipline. Different subjects do, of course, share command words; but it is very important to note that shared words doesn't necessarily imply shared understanding of what those words mean. For example, to 'evaluate' in an English task means 'State how you react when reading the text' as in 'Evaluate the effects the descriptions have on you', whereas in maths it means 'Identify which part of the method, calculation or assertion is incorrect, or explain why it must be correct'. Knowing the different requirements of the command words in each discipline will help students join the language dots – and this is another reason why it is so important that language awareness policy be a whole-school affair, and not something confined to subject silos.

There is an increasing demand for children to write extended answers in all subjects, even the traditionally numerate ones, such as maths and the sciences, so there is an increasing need for them to be able to express themselves in all subjects. In the next chapter we will be addressing the whole question of metalanguage, SPaG, or 'teaching grammar'. For now, though, let us just note that although children are taught metalanguage at KS2, they need to be reminded of its importance at all Key Stages. As literacy blogger James Durran says: '[Explicit grammar knowledge] will be particularly useful when teaching writing: in any subject, a shared language with which to refer to the structure of a sentence, to types of word and to the function of these things in expression is invaluable when editing writing, when teaching forms of writing and when investigating, practising and breaking free from different genres – not just in English, but across the curriculum.'[19] The implication of this is very clear. It demands a universal approach across the school to language: if each department uses the same terminology, students will be able to identify and use that language across the curriculum.

4.4 Conclusion

In this chapter we have made the case for teachers being encouraged to be more language aware. English teachers have a direct responsibility for laying the foundations of linguistic knowledge so that children can identify and understand the linguistic links between each subject, but all teachers share the responsibility for developing that knowledge. After all, it doesn't really matter whether the text we're looking at is a Shakespeare sonnet or an explanation of plate tectonics. What we're interested in is how the writer uses language: how they achieve their desired communicative effect. In this sense, all classrooms are language classrooms and English is no different from any other subject.

What we are essentially doing here is borrowing from the approach to communication which linguists tend to associate with M. A. K. Halliday and social semiotics, and which for our purposes can be summed up, in an admittedly simplistic fashion, as selecting from your linguistic resources in order to achieve the desired communicative effect for a specific audience. It is demonstrably a more nuanced approach to academic writing than 'you have to select the right words from this list' – i.e. the most academic-looking or most obscure – or as we saw earlier, 'avoid two-word verbs'. Perhaps more importantly, though, it obliges children to concentrate on the objective of their writing, and to think in terms of genre (see the Text Box earlier), and how skilled writers shape and adapt their language to the context.

As we noted just now, of course, making links between subjects is crucial, so that children know what they're doing in terms of writing and speaking, why and when, whether they are in a biology class or a maths one. In the next chapter, though, we turn our attention to what goes on in English lessons. We will argue that English departments also need to become more language-aware in order to unify the different strands of what is taught in English lessons in secondary schools.

Notes

1 Cited in Goddard, A. (2012), *Doing English Language: A Guide For Students*. London & New York: Routledge, p. 4.
2 Treffers-Daller, J. & Milton, J. (2013), 'Vocabulary size revisited: the link between vocabulary size and academic achievement'. *Applied Linguistics Review* 4(1): 151–172.
3 Sussex dialect words for a green woodpecker and yew berries respectively, in case you're wondering.
4 https://global.oup.com/education/content/dictionaries/key-issues/word-gap/?region=uk
5 https://www.englishandmedia.co.uk/blog/the-value-of-talk-or-how-we-need-to-use-new-words-to-learn-new-words
6 The popular 'tiers' model labels much of the vocabulary found predominantly in written text, or in the speech of mature speakers, as 'Tier 2'. 'Tier 1' is the everyday language that rarely needs formal teaching, while 'Tier 3' is domain- or subject-specific technical vocabulary. See Beck, I., McKeown, M. & Kucan, L. (2013), *Bringing Words to Life* (2nd edition). New York: Guilford.
7 https://www.tes.com/teaching-resource/key-word-lists-for-as-and-a2-aqa-biology-11523933
8 Mortimore, K. (2020), *Disciplinary Literacy and Explicit Vocabulary Teaching: A Whole School Approach to Closing the Attainment Gap*. Melton: John Catt Educational.
9 Martínez, E., Mollica, F. & Gibson, E. (2022), 'Poor writing, not specialized concepts, drives processing difficulty in legal language'. *Cognition* 224. DOI: 10.1016/j.cognition.2022.105070
10 https://socialsciences.exeter.ac.uk/education/research/centres/writing/grammar-teacher-resources/grammaraschoice/thegrammarforwritingpedagogy/
11 Macrae, A. (2016), 'Stylistics'. In Giovanelli, M. & Clayton, D., *Knowing About Language: Linguistics and the Secondary English Classroom*. London: Routledge, pp. 51–63.

12 Giovanelli, M. (2016), 'The value of linguistics to the teacher'. Also in Giovanelli & Clayton (2016), pp. 13–24.

13 Clayton, D. & McCallum, A. (2018), *KS3 Language Laboratory*. London: English and Media Centre.

14 English, F. (2011), *Student Writing and Genre*. London: Bloomsbury. [Originally published by Continuum].

15 Collins, S. (2021), 'Teaching sentence level analysis in fictional texts'. In Ahmed, F., Giovanelli, M., Mansworth, M. & Titjen, F. *Teaching English Language and Literature 16–19*. Abingdon and New York: Routledge, pp. 18–25.

16 AQA English Literature GCSE Paper 1, June 2017.

17 2021 Assessment Resources, 8462 GCSE Chemistry (Accessed online).

18 2021 Assessment Resources, 8461 GCSE Biology (Accessed online).

19 https://jamesdurran.blog/2018/07/12/fear-of-grammar-and-the-grammar-of-fear/

PART II
Language as subject

What we teach when we teach English

5.1 Introduction: 'Here comes English!'

Every now and again, I (Steve) have cause to visit the Design and Technology faculty at my school. The Head of Department there and I have a long-running spot of repartee whereby he will call out, to patient grins from the students:

> Oh, here comes English! Mind your p's and q's now, kids. We've got to speak proper! Mind your language!

And I will then reply with something flippant and probably mistaken about dovetail joints or something. It's good fun, and it's all meant in jest, of course, but it does say something about the way English teachers are often positioned. English teachers are seen as the people who model correct usage: they are there at least in part to guard and uphold the quality of the language, to encourage everyone to 'speak proper' and not let standards slip. Regardless of how English teachers themselves feel about that positioning, or how it compares to the reality of the job, it is a common assumption that it is the English teachers who should be a school's experts in reading, writing and speaking. But is that really what we are? And what else are we? Are we primarily the professional spelling, punctuation and grammar 'sticklers' – or do we like to think we are more the kind of people who set author Ian McEwan on the path to be able to say: 'Studying English literature at school was my first and probably my biggest step towards mental freedom and independence. It was like falling in love with life'?

This chapter is all about the role of English teachers in schools: what it is that we do, what everyone thinks we do, and how we can improve it. To this end, we take a brief historical detour to explain how English became two different but related subjects – English language and English literature, with the literature part of it often privileged over the language. We explore the current state of the English curriculum, what works and what needs changing, and the role that English departments can play in making schools places of critical language awareness. We ask

DOI: 10.4324/9781003201281-7

whether the idea of 'English' is actually well understood, now that the most recent prescriptive reforms have arguably made English a less engaging subject for teachers and pupils, with the consequence that A level entries are falling fast. We make the case for teaching spelling and grammar in a contextualised, language-aware way; and, finally, we suggest that schools might be able to address the decline by putting language awareness at the front and centre of the whole school, not just the English classroom.

5.2 The experts who aren't always experts: English teachers and language

What pupils study in English has changed quite dramatically since the reforms of the National Curriculum in 2013. One *very* notable change has been the progressively greater emphasis placed on grammar. In the years after these reforms were first implemented, it wasn't unusual to notice that children starting secondary school in Year 7 knew more about language and grammar than those who were completing GCSE courses and starting A Level English Language. It is surely to be welcomed that from an early age children should begin to be taught to think about how language works. And so as far as we can see, there is nothing wrong with the National Curriculum teaching grammar at KS2 – provided that it is taught in a language-aware, contextualised way, with a focus on function and meaning, not as a series of unconnected rules and terms to be memorised. But it is too often the case that primary school children are merely taught how to identify language features, rather than how to understand them or appreciate the way they function in communication.

Some of the KS2 English tests, particularly the much-discussed SPaG test, have appeared to encourage this emphasis on identification rather than explanation of key features of the English language. The heavily technical focus of the tests loomed larger than usual in the public consciousness in 2021, when most children were unable to go to school during the Covid pandemic. Many parents, obliged to get involved with their children's online learning, soon complained that it was very hard to help their ten- and eleven-year-olds with English when they had no idea what a 'fronted adverbial' was. Journalists and novelists with children, meanwhile, proudly proclaimed that they had managed to make a decent living as wordsmiths without ever being able to recognise a fronted adverbial if one had stared them in the face. As one newspaper column written by a novelist and mother put it: 'Fronted adverbials be damned. Let's teach the young what really matters.'

It is, of course, easy to understand that parents found grammar teaching challenging, especially when they were probably not taught much grammar themselves. However, it is not at all uncommon to find secondary school teachers similarly in the dark, or at least lacking in confidence about explicit language teaching, when they hadn't been taught systematically about language, either. Most secondary English teachers – nearly all of them, in fact – have degrees in English literature, not English language or linguistics; it is natural that they tend to feel intellectually more at home with Jane Austen than they do with Noam Chomsky, and as a general rule they feel more comfortable with narrative and poetic voices than they do with formal linguistic analysis. Nor is it necessarily just that they lack confidence or interest. Professor of linguistics Richard Hudson has pointed to research which suggests that a fair number of secondary English teachers are unconvinced about the actual value of teaching the structure of language, and question the validity of the whole undertaking. In recent years English teachers seem to have become steadily more adept at delivering linguistic content and skills, but it still often feels that they would rather be focusing their pupils' minds on novels, poems and plays. They might be right, of course: a recent study (heavily criticised, we should note) by the Nuffield Foundation suggested that the National Curriculum's focus on grammar teaching had a negligible impact on primary school children's ability to write stories, for example.

So, as we have already suggested, despite the popular image of English teachers being beady-eyed sticklers for correctness, in fact quite a lot of them are not really 'language experts' at all or, rather, not in the way many people think they are. In fact, they might even be unsure of the basics. To illustrate the point, let's return (very briefly, we promise!) to the question of Standard English, which we discussed in Chapters 2 and 3. When we were working on those chapters, Steve carried out a little straw poll of English teachers, asking what they understood by the term 'Standard English'. The replies varied spectacularly. Some were clearly knowledgeable and nuanced, like this one:

A conventionally accepted set of practices in, largely, written English.

Or this one, which emphasised the vital distinction between accent and grammatical form:

Standard spoken English leans towards the formal, for the purpose of communicating clearly. Therefore, slang will be avoided. What standard spoken English is NOT: Queen's English or southern accented English. Though speakers of standard spoken English may have a southern accent.

Others, though, fell in line with the notion of 'standard = correct':

Standard written English... is grammatically correct and punctuated so that it makes sense.

And for some, there persisted confusion between standard grammar and the RP accent:

English that does not use slang or colloquialisms, considered formal in line with Received Pronunciation.

English teachers are the language professionals tasked with leading the push for explicit language knowledge and with building cultural capital by encouraging standard grammar in speech, but a good many of them make heavy weather of explaining clearly or accurately what Standard English actually is. And could most English teachers define with precision the difference between colloquialisms and slang, say, or between slang and dialect? Regardless of your views on the rights and wrongs of the policies involved, it's really a rather odd state of affairs. Anecdotally, a fair number of English teachers seem to have gained more insight into the mechanics of language from doing a TEFL qualification (such as the CELTA or DELTA) than they did from their English degrees. In fact, one teacher suggested to us that, just as all new teachers need to demonstrate a competency in English and maths, every English teacher should have at least rudimentary knowledge of another language, so that they understand how language, any language, works. Effective teaching about language, demonstrably, relies entirely on language awareness among teachers. We plan to say a good deal more about this later in this chapter, but for now, let us spend a little time laying out the 'English' journey which all children in England and Wales embark upon.

5.3 Language awareness is at the heart of what we do in 'English'

At Key Stage 3 everyone studies English as one subject, the subject of English having morphed from 'Literacy' at primary school. Then at Key Stage 4 children are suddenly prepared for two separate GCSEs taught by English specialists: English Language and English Literature. Children tend to find this confusing – and why wouldn't they? Everyone knows what history and geography are about. Everyone knows what the sciences are about (there used to be an old teachers' joke about school lab experiments that went: 'If it moves it's biology, if it changes it's chemistry, and if it doesn't work, it's physics'), and most people think they know what maths is about (at least until it starts getting advanced and abstract). But what is English about? What do we teach when we teach English? And why is this attempt to define ourselves so difficult? Partly it's because everyone has different ideas about what we do. Like the colleague who jokingly thinks he needs to 'mind his language' in an English teacher's presence, parents and school management can be uncertain about what our primary responsibilities are. But sometimes, as we shall see, we even end up at odds with each other.

So what exactly is 'English' about? It's certainly about at least two very different things – the study of language and the study of literature. In fact, you could make a reasonable case for the subject of English being four quite distinct things:

- learning to write using, predominantly, Standard English grammar

- learning how to express yourself effectively and appropriately, in speaking and writing

- learning grammatical terminology, the 'parts of speech' or SPaG

- reading and evaluating works of literature written in English

And actually, there's a fifth, which is not quite like the others, but it's the one that drives many literature graduates to want to dedicate their lives to teaching:

- understanding, through literature, what it means to be human

And then there's EAL, of course – the teaching of English as a second language to children, often recent immigrants, who speak another language at home. It's obviously an English-related subject, but what does it have in common with the traditional 'core' elements of the English classroom? In some ways it is more akin to MFL teaching, but in many schools it is not even taught by a language specialist – assuming anyone formally 'teaches' it at all, rather than it being simply the province of an assistant, a volunteer or an ad hoc member of support staff.

But what do all of the above have in common? Is there genuine coherence here, or are these wildly different things, which have been bundled together through historical accident and all labelled 'English' for the sake of convenience? Well, we would suggest that 'English' as a subject only has coherence when we acknowledge and understand that at the heart of *all* that we do is language awareness. Without an awareness of language, children will not understand how to communicate effectively or how others, peers or Shakespeare, communicate with them. So English teachers, even literature specialists, need to think of themselves and position themselves as language awareness professionals. This kind of shift in thinking, if it happened at a national policy level, could also help lend coherence to the confusion that currently afflicts KS3 and GCSE English, leading to declining pupil engagement and poor take-up at A Level.

Beyond the subject 'English', we believe it is also a major responsibility of the language-aware English teacher to help drive the development of language awareness across the school, bringing language awareness into other subjects and advising on whole-school language policy and practice. We will return to this in our final chapter – but in order to create the space for this language-aware environment, it might be helpful to explain how we got to a position where the teaching of English can actually be a place devoid of, or seriously lacking in, language awareness. We will argue that English teaching has always been caught between the Scylla of moral improvement and cultural identity provided by English literature, and the Charybdis of the prescriptive naming of grammar parts, and that this has led to a lack of clarity in what is actually taught and why it is taught. So let's take a quick historical detour.

5.4 English language, English literature: Frankenstein? Or Jekyll and Hyde?

It seems hard to imagine now, but English as a school subject is relatively young, only really having been taught since the late nineteenth century. Before the

Education Reform Act of 1870, those lucky enough to receive any substantial education, mainly the upper and middle classes, would study the classical languages,
which were believed to be at the heart of humanistic and liberal education. The
1870 Act paved the way for the establishment of maintained schools, which, as
Louise Poulson explains in her *The English Curriculum in Schools*,[1] would provide a 'cheap and basic education' based around the rudiments of the three Rs for
the newly enfranchised lower and middle classes following the 1867 Reform Act.
The then Chancellor of the Exchequer, Robert Lowe, suggested that English was
vital to 'educate our masters', by which he meant that if middle- and working-class
men – it was only men – were to be involved in the democratic process, then they
needed at least to be literate.

There was little or no mention of literature, and, indeed, as late as the early
twentieth century, English literature was generally regarded as something suitable
only for women to study as an academic subject, or for men to read for pleasure. In
1921, though, the Newbolt Committee, set up to look at post-World War I educational provision, approvingly echoed Mathew Arnold's view that literature played
a central role in moral and civil education. The everyday spoken language of the
working classes, meanwhile, was regarded as largely deficient (as well as divisive,
in the sense that it seemed almost as if different social classes spoke different languages). The committee's report therefore recommended the explicit teaching of
Standard English, by which 'uncivilised' usage and 'barbarisms' were to be eradi-
cated in the speech of working-class children.

So for the first part of the twentieth century, literature was promoted as being
socially and morally valuable, and as a way of promoting a national (but mainly
English) identity. Language teaching, predictably enough, was cheerfully and
unapologetically prescriptive: it concentrated on 'right' and 'wrong' ways of speaking and writing, and grammar teaching consisted mainly of the decontextualised
naming of parts – a practice which has recently been revived at KS2, as we mentioned above. Not that there weren't concerted efforts to encourage a more systematic analysis of language use, later in the century. The *Language for Life* paper (DES
1975), known as the Bullock Report, recommended that all schools have a language
policy and that all trainee teachers be taught about language (we return to this idea
in Chapter 8); as a result, the National Congress of Languages in Education was
created to promote language awareness. There were other developments in later
years, which we won't go into in any detail: notably, the Kingsman Report (1988)
which encouraged language analysis and the study of language development and
language variation, giving rise to the establishment of the Language in the National
Curriculum (LINC) project in 1989. LINC did produce a package of teaching materials in 1992, but these were ultimately withdrawn (a fate met by other similar projects) because, according to Deborah Cameron, there were 'too many references to
class, race and gender and too permissive a line on grammar'. The last, particularly,
sounds very likely indeed. Nevertheless, their unofficial dissemination through

sympathetic teachers, as Marcello Giovanelli has pointed out, ultimately gave rise to the current A Level English Language.

But we're getting ahead of ourselves. By the mid-twentieth century, the historical development of the subject had settled down into a recognisable shape. On the one hand was the world of literature, which spoke of moral uplift, aesthetics and the Great Tradition. At the extreme of this view of the discipline lay the idea of 'English' as glamour: stars of university English departments, like the Leavises, attracted coteries of devoted admirers and hosted literary salons. You can easily imagine cocktail parties on college lawns and passionate debates in seminars and senior common rooms. The language side of it, though, was very far from glamorous, with the more exciting-seeming language work taking place in departments of philosophy and the newly-created departments of linguistics. Indeed, for ambitious young English graduates beginning a teaching career, it might have looked a bit utilitarian and lacking in creativity: did it perhaps still conjure up images of correcting the grammar of working class children in their hobnailed boots?

We still see the faint outlines of this historical division in the subject, even today. Most English teachers took, and still take, degrees specialising in literature; relatively few have been enthused by the prospect of teaching grammar. So, with the tradition of English being taught by literature specialists, and the explicit teaching of language being relatively new (or newly resurrected), and by no means universally welcomed or even accepted, there is still a sense nowadays that English language is the poor cousin in English teaching. Language specialists are sometimes regarded by literary types as 'rude mechanicals', rather than creatives. At a well-respected university in the north of England, one linguist friend of ours jokes of his department: 'It's called the English department, but English is always spelled with a silent L-I-T-....' There seems to be, though, a welcome change in the air at present, as English teachers become more language-aware and better equipped to teach language-focused lessons. We'll say a bit more about this later in the chapter, when we discuss the situation at English A Level, but for now we turn our attention to an area which raises questions which affect whole-school policy: namely, the teaching of spelling, punctuation and grammar (SPaG).

5.5 Can we learn to love SPaG?

We've already discussed the resistance to explicit grammar teaching: many of us who are older than, say, about 40, studied English without any real focus on the technical aspects of language. And it's true that there are many people who don't understand how grammar works, but are good writers and are perfectly well able to communicate. There are two issues here: teaching the rudiments of grammar might switch anyone off; and it may well justifiably have been abandoned in schools for a long time. Equally, sceptical parents and teachers surely make a reasonable point when they challenge the current logic of teaching a 10-year-old to recognise the subjunctive, for instance.

At Key Stages 1, 2 and 3 children are taught the rudiments of spelling, punctuation and grammar. At the end of KS2, children will have to sit a SPaG test, which produces a fair amount of dread when mentioned (or when mentioned to adults, anyway). Actually, children are taught far more than the rudiments. The teachers' glossary for the programmes of study for English in the National Curriculum runs to 18 pages and covers everything from the active voice to word families, including definitions of participles and split digraphs along the way. By the time children sit their GCSE exams, they are awarded a total of 32 marks for their 'technical accuracy' as it is called at KS4, worth one-fifth of their GCSE grade.

The renewed emphasis on 'grammar', however that is understood, and especially the SPaG test, have come in for a good deal of criticism. Some of this criticism is certainly warranted – however, we don't think that grammar teaching is in itself a bad thing. Why do people working with language need to identify and name grammatical items? For the same reason that mechanics or doctors need to be able to identify car or body parts, basically: it's to enable us to talk precisely and economically about how language works, without needing to explain ourselves laboriously at every turn. Metalanguage – the language we use to talk about language – is a professional tool. Anything that helps us work with language more effectively is to be welcomed, and we therefore embrace the teaching of spelling, punctuation and grammar as the basic building blocks of written language awareness.

So what's the problem? Well, the problem with SPaG in the curriculum as it stands at present is that it represents a job half done, because while it demands the learning of grammatical terms and items, it fails to complete the picture by showing what this grammar can *do*. And while a lot of effort is put into teaching identification of terminology at KS2, this is not built upon or developed into teaching the understanding of functions of grammar terms at KS3 and KS4.

Knowing what the passive voice is (or a modal verb, or an adverbial phrase, for that matter) might not in itself be useful. What is useful is being able to recognise and understand the functions of the passive voice in, for example, concealing agency (see our discussion of newspaper headlines in just a moment), foregrounding a particular subject in a clause, or expressing authority. Or take the crucial role of the much-maligned 'fronted adverbial' in academic writing, where it allows the writer to indicate an attitudinal stance in relation to a following statement ('Curiously, the armistice did not come into force until 11 o'clock that day'). Knowing what a fronted adverbial is, is an essential prerequisite for understanding and talking about what it can do.

Once a child has a basic grounding in grammar, as well as being able to explain what a writer is doing, they can experiment with different grammatical effects when they are writing themselves, in the way that an artist might test out different styles and colours. The linguist David Crystal uses an example from Terry Pratchett's novel *The Carpet People* to illustrate this, when the character Pismire sees 'the gleam of ten thousand eyes, green, red and white'.[2] Placing the adjectives after the noun and at the end of a sentence in this way, argues Crystal, has the effect of building a sense of unease and fear. In my own lessons I (Steve) often talk about the 'Yoda effect' whereby playing with the word order of a sentence, as the Star Wars character does, can totally change the emphasis of the words ('Save you, it can'). This type of detailed language work can *only* be done if children have been taught what the individual grammar components and their functions are. Even at the most basic level, you can only talk about the position of adjectives and nouns if you are clear about what adjectives and nouns are.

One of the ways we teach children how to be critical, careful readers is to ask them to consider the particular lexical and grammatical choices made by a writer, and what communicative effect these choices have. Take these two examples of how verbs are used in different ways to represent the same news story. A 2018 headline on the *New York Times* website read: 'Dozens of Palestinians have died in protests as the US prepares to open its Jerusalem Embassy'. The *Wall Street Journal*, meanwhile, reported: 'Scores killed as Palestinians protest US Embassy opening in Jerusalem'. Notice how in the *New York Times* headline, the Palestinians simply 'died'. That headline caused outrage on social media because it seemed to imply that Palestinians had not been killed as a result of clashes with the Israeli security forces. The second headline, here using an elliptical form of the passive voice ('scores killed' being newspaper headline-speak for 'scores have been killed' or 'scores were killed'), makes it more obvious that Palestinian protesters died due to clashes with security forces – but it still does not anywhere acknowledge that those security forces were responsible.

By exploring the different ways that stories are reported in the news, children are being introduced to Critical Discourse Analysis, which uses language awareness to help them to understand how the media may want to foreground a particular aspect of a news story. But again, let's be clear: this detailed, critical reading is only possible once the preliminary grammar work has been done.

5.5.1 Punctuation and spelling

And it is not just grammar that needs to be 'taught' rather than 'caught' as the old phrase goes; the same can be said for punctuation. Recognising how punctuation can change meaning is something that is taught at KS2. The well-known example of how an omitted comma can be used to change the line

'Let's eat, Grandma!'
to
'Let's eat Grandma!'

is one that most children will be able to remember, because it's fun. But the important thing is that this basic knowledge will be built on later to show, in the context of literature, for example, how poets use a caesura for dramatic effect, or how Emily Dickinson uses dashes in her poetry. The English and Media Centre's (EMC's) KS3 Language Laboratory[3] explores the links between punctuation and emojis and explains how punctuation, like all other aspects of language, is constantly changing. Class-based discussions about whether new forms of punctuation are required (like some of the newer conventions of text message punctuation) can actually make for stimulating lessons, as children learn for themselves how punctuation works and, most importantly, what it does.

And while 'spelling' might conjure up for children grim tests for which they are forced to learn long lists of irrelevant and unconnected words, this needn't be the case. Like grammar and punctuation, spelling can provide us with another sample to put under the language awareness microscope. Historical context can help here. David Crystal explains: 'to understand the complexity of English spelling, we first have to understand when and how the language was originally written down'.[4] To cut a very long story short, he shows that English spelling derives from a number of key events, including: the recording of Anglo-Saxon by Christian monks in the sixth century; the introduction of French words and changes in pronunciation following the Norman invasion in 1066; the Great Vowel Shift and the establishment of the east Midlands dialect as the standard; the introduction of printing and the standardisation of spelling in the seventeenth century; and the expansion of trade and establishment of empire.

Nevertheless, in spite of all these disparate influences, 75 per cent of English words are actually spelt regularly; it's the other quarter we have to worry about, but you could argue that that's what makes English so interesting! Once children start to understand where English spelling comes from – once they begin to see that even untypical spellings are not just random assemblages of letters – they will be better placed to recognise the patterns and systems which will help them to make fewer spelling mistakes. And the usefulness of having a grasp of the basics of etymology and morphology, so children understand how word formation happens, stretches across disciplines. In short, language-aware English teachers embrace spelling, punctuation and grammar, and teach them in context and from a functional perspective.

5.5.2 Resisting the resistance to grammar teaching

Let's try and respond to some of the common objections to explicit grammar teaching in the English classroom.

I don't like imposing rules, as I want the children to be free to express themselves creatively.

For a long time many English teachers didn't feel comfortable teaching syntax rules, punctuation, when to use the passive voice and when not to. But why? To be interested in rules, such as grammar rules, is not to be anti-free expression, or to negate creativity. Rules are part of the package of language, the engine that makes language work (linguists refer to this property of language as 'generativity': the grammar rules allow you to generate an infinite number of meaningful utterances and sentences). So language specialists look at the rules, not in order to impose them mechanically, but in order to understand and explain what they do. Haiku has strict parameters of acceptability (the five-seven-five syllable pattern), as do the sonnet (fourteen lines), Aristotelian dramatic conventions (three acts) and the twelve-bar blues (the clue's in the name!). But no one thinks that artists working within these traditions lack creativity or freedom of expression. We look at form and recognise that what writers do within the accepted constraints of the form is part of what makes them creative.

> *I don't really understand the point of it. I got away without knowing it and I still love literature.*

This view tends to be heard most from those teachers who were never taught grammar themselves, and reflects the views of many of the English literature graduates who go into teaching. As I mentioned above, some of my English teacher colleagues have admitted that they don't like teaching language because 'it's so dry'. So they know that they don't like it – but it's not at all certain that they really know what 'grammar' in the linguistic sense actually is. They often have very stereotypical and negative views of it, tending to associate it with rigid orthodoxy, prescriptivism and old-fashioned teaching methods. This is an ongoing real issue, which fortunately is beginning to be addressed by awarding bodies and education trainers. AQA, the UK's largest examination board with 61 per cent of the market share of examination candidates, offers training to literature specialists to prepare them for teaching A Level English Language, and the EMC offers a selection of courses for English teachers which focus on teaching grammar in context. And this is surely the key to the whole problem: grammar study must be situated firmly within the wider study of language.

> *Grammar is unnecessary – students don't need to know it.*

Well – there are lots of things you learn at school that could be regarded as unnecessary. You almost certainly don't need equations, and you probably won't ever need French, as we will discuss in the next chapter. There is little point in attaching value to school subjects per se – it is how they shape your mind and make you see your world that is invaluable. And just because you didn't learn grammar, for instance, doesn't mean that others shouldn't! The pursuit of knowledge is part of what makes life meaningful; the fact that you don't know about Russian formalism or bacteriology doesn't mean that they are not worth knowing. But in any case, we would argue that some knowledge of grammar is a hugely useful, practical asset for any child (or indeed adult).

I (Tim) had the task some years ago at an east London comprehensive school of teaching beginner's German to a class of teenagers, none of whom had ever been taught grammar in any systematic way, using a textbook which proudly claimed that it could help you learn German 'without complicated grammatical explanations'. It was not, to put it mildly, an experience I would be keen to repeat. How do you explain that definite articles (like *der, die, dem*) vary according to grammatical gender, number and case, to children who don't know what gender, number, case or indeed articles are? How do you explain that the preposition *auf* sometimes takes the dative case and sometimes the accusative, to people who have never previously heard the words preposition, dative or accusative? It must be just about possible to learn German without explicit grammatical knowledge and without grammatical explanations (German children manage it, after all), but it would take a very, very long time and require a massive amount of exposure – as indeed it does for German children, or for any children acquiring their mother tongue (see our discussion of children and language learning at Section 7.4.1 in Chapter 7). Learning the technical terms might be a laborious business, but once done, it puts a booster under children's all-round language development, in both English and foreign languages, enabling them to think and speak with precision and economy about how language works.

We're interested in language and linguistics, and talking about language forms a big part of what we do every day. So of course from our point of view it's encouraging that there is this new focus on grammar and metalanguage (the language we use to talk about language). But – and it's quite a big but – they have to be taught well. That is, they have to be taught in a way that is accessible, appealing and engaging. While stories abound about how teachers and parents struggle to get their own heads round complex grammatical terms, there is a real opportunity now to promote language awareness to young people. Teachers and parents are perhaps only just beginning to realise that by teaching children how language actually *works*, they will become better at language. They will be able to recognise that language is primarily about resources and how we use them, rather than primarily about rules and why we must obey them.

And one last thing. We would argue that the only way to really understand language *and* literature is by understanding how language works at all levels, and while there remains this breach between these two areas of English study, we are not doing our job as English teachers properly. As we suggested in Section 5.3, the key to mending the breach, or restoring cohesion to the subject, is understanding that it is at heart a language awareness issue. But to what extent is language awareness built into the curriculum? In fact, how is language dealt with in the National Curriculum?

5.6 Language in the National Curriculum

We're going to explore how the English curriculum looks at the different stages of a child's progress through the system, or what is now sometimes called the 'learning journey': first Key Stage 3, followed by Key Stage 4 and the GCSE exams, then A Level.

5.6.1 The picture at Key Stage 3

The picture at KS3 is of an opportunity missed, because of a serious lack of continuity with what has come before. As we noted above, since the 2013 reforms to the National Curriculum there has been a renewed focus on grammar at KS2, albeit in a largely prescriptive manner. Unfortunately, however, the same cannot be said for KS3. Often, in fact, the groundwork laid in primary schools is neglected or even ignored. This might be because of the supposed streamlining of content in the Programme of Study at KS3; Dan Clayton calls it a 'stripped-down' programme, which has squeezed the wider study of language out of the picture. But equally, it might also be because the teachers delivering English at secondary level are not so well versed in the importance of grammar, or are not convinced of its relevance to the study of 'English'. In any case, it is plain that the lack of a coherent pathway from one Key Stage to the next means that the earlier study of grammar is not currently built upon, and is not allowed to develop and blossom into a wider understanding of how language works. Moreover, with the introduction of 'life after levels' following the abandonment of the SATs, there were two further, connected consequences: first, the leaching of GCSE tasks down into KS3, and then an accompanying narrowing of the written tasks being assessed at KS3. Gone were the tasks based on writing triplets, such as *analyse, review, comment* and *imagine, explore, entertain.* This is a great pity.

However, to look on the bright side, it might be that there's an opportunity here to develop some explicit, but contextualised grammar teaching in the secondary English classroom, made easier by the fact that children will be prepared for it. In a survey carried out by Jennifer Webb of Funky Pedagogy, just over half of the secondary English teachers polled acknowledged the importance of grammar teaching but admitted they didn't do it, while nearly 10 per cent believed that grammar teaching was 'not important'. This is not to say, though, that there isn't an increasing awareness of the place of grammar in English teaching, or that there isn't growing support on hand to help teachers develop their skills in this area. The EMC, for example, offers training on how to teach grammar in context at KS3, while its *Language Laboratory* textbook provides schemes of work across the three years of KS3 including units on language in literature, creating a voice through creative grammar, and language change. There are also excellent resources available from universities (e.g. Exeter and UCL) as well as educational publishers such as Collins, with their *Crafting Brilliant Sentences* by Lindsay Skinner. In short, it just might be that the picture is beginning to improve.

5.6.2 The picture at Key Stage 4

As with KS3, at KS4 there has been a considerable narrowing-down of the kinds of writing demanded of students, and they are now only required to *describe, entertain, argue or persuade.* With this narrowing, regrettably, there has been a further loss of language awareness, for if a child is less familiar with a variety of writing forms, they are naturally less aware of the possible range of different communicative contexts. Some schools will ensure that a fuller range of communicative events is studied and that communicative resources (in terms not just of grammar, but of discourse and register, or appropriacy to context) are taught. But of course it won't always happen, as schools struggle with the demands of a limited but still challenging GCSE.

Because of the pressure to meet the demands of what is actually now a more difficult syllabus, some school English departments might find themselves 'teaching to test' at GCSE. This results in a drier, less appealing learning experience for children, which in turn has a negative impact on recruitment to study English at KS5.

5.6.3 The current state of the English Language GCSE exam

In 2019, the EMC's survey of teachers showed that only a small minority of teachers had anything positive to say about the English language GCSE. There are doubtless many reasons for this, but it is more than likely that one of them is the exam's failure to engage in detail with the question of language. We would argue that although the GCSE in English Language does feature language analysis, it does not succeed in developing in students the kind of wider language awareness that we believe should be at the centre of English teaching – indeed, it sometimes hardly seems to try.

What pupils currently study in English Language lessons is a hybrid of reading comprehension, inference, synthesis and evaluation, along with the two (quite limited) creative writing tasks we mentioned above. There is no doubt that these are all useful skills, and will help them to negotiate at least some of the texts and communicative events that they encounter in the real world. However, while it is clear that they are learning how language is *used*, in order to recognise a (limited) variety of communicative events, it is not clear that they are learning explicitly about how language *works*. This view was given considerable weight by the large-scale survey carried out in 2021 by the National Association for the Teaching of English (NATE), which has been campaigning for a reform of the English Language GCSE for some time now. Its report declares:

> To prepare young people for life and learning in the 21st century, NATE believes that GCSE English Language should offer an informed understanding and competent use of the multiple modes and functions of language in the contemporary world.

It goes on to recommend that:

> [The GCSE] should also act as a preparation for the well-established A Level English Language courses for those who wish to study language at a higher level.

In addition, it recommends that the following changes, among others, should be made to the GCSE:

- Include greater variety of writing tasks, including textual intervention

- Opportunities to study language, including theory

- Study of spoken language and knowledge about language

- Inclusion of more modern texts, including media and multimodal

- Make GCSE an actual study of language in the modern world, including e.g. accent and dialect

And there is an explicit demand that 'Students should explore varieties of spoken language as used in different contexts, including the language of those from other cultural backgrounds, allowing for a wide range of talk repertoires'.

These recommendations seem to us to be exactly the kinds of areas of study which will help develop language awareness. Through negotiating multimodal texts, re-focusing on speaking and listening, acquiring some sociolinguistic background, appreciating the significance of writing for different purposes, and being exposed to a more diverse set of texts in which language is used for different communicative effects, students will be better qualified to negotiate a wider variety of language events.

5.6.4 The current state of English at A Level

The background we have traced from KS2 onwards leads inexorably to some of the current problems being experienced with recruitment at English A Level. As Marcello Giovanelli puts it:

> Despite a renewed focus on grammar at KS2, the latest reforms at KS3 and KS4 fail to provide a coherent pathway from KS2 to KS5 work, and may also mean that many students will not do any meaningful language-based study across their five years in secondary school.

It is perhaps little surprise, then, that since 2017 the number of students choosing to study A Level Language has dropped from 21,000 to 14,000. Students who have done no meaningful language-based work in their secondary school careers are unlikely to suddenly develop a strong desire to do A Level English Language. But that can't be the whole story – because in the same time frame, the number of students opting to study A Level English Literature has fallen from 42,000 to 33,000, while those opting for A Level Language and Literature has dropped from 10,000 to 7,000. The recruitment problem affects the whole suite of English A Levels.

Now, there may be a number of reasons for this: the removal of the AS option could be one factor; the increased popularity of STEM subjects is probably another.

Although English Literature remains the most popular English A Level to study, even this subject has recorded a fall in numbers. But it is the drop in students studying A Level English Language which is most worrying; and at school, it can be a challenge to recruit A Level language teachers or encourage literature specialists to teach the subject. In my own experience (Steve), as noted at Section 5.5.2 above, colleagues with English literature degrees claim they find A Level English Language too dry, technical, too full of jargon, or just not that interesting compared to teaching literature. But I suspect the problem might be that they just don't really know what the subject entails. Perhaps it needs rebranding? As plenty of commentators have pointed out, a lot of what is covered in the course could comfortably be accommodated under the umbrella description of linguistics or applied linguistics. Once teachers realise that the course really isn't just 'grammar' or dull technical terms, while they might still be taken out of their comfort zone, they often become fascinated by it.

The negative attitude to language and grammar is not helped by a persistent perception that English Language has less kudos than English Literature. In 2019, the Russell Group of universities ditched the category of 'facilitating subjects': the sciences, history, geography, languages, maths and English – from its recommendations for A Level study. An urban myth had emerged that these were the A Level subjects which would be viewed most favourably by the top universities. However, research found that there was no evidence to suggest that A Levels on the facilitating subjects list were any more favoured than those not on the list, and the Russell Group said that it was 'never the case' that one A Level was preferred over another.

Perceptions of difficulty and suitability of A Level subjects are hard to break down. A former Head of Department at my school wanted to replace English Language and Literature with A Level Language, because she believed that the combined course was too academically challenging for the type of students it attracted, and that English Language was a better fit for them. While Literature tends to attract students with higher Alps targets than those studying A Level Language, the latter course is just as demanding as the Literature and the Language and Literature courses. It requires students to study texts (*any* texts!) from the seventeenth century to the modern day, plus sociolinguistics and language acquisition; then to write for a variety of audiences, conduct an investigation into an aspect of language of their choice, and produce some original writing and write a commentary on it. No one course is easier than the others: they are just different. As an A Level Language teacher, I have seen students achieve A* grades in all three subjects they have studied and go on to Russell Group universities.

5.7 Conclusion: back to language awareness

We began this chapter by noting that English teachers inhabit a number of different roles, and we've explored some of the fractures and challenges inherent in a subject which is called, simply, 'English' but which is actually composed of multiple strands. What ties it all together, though, is the notion of the English teacher as language specialist, with a central role in developing language awareness across the discipline and across the school. Language awareness can unite language and literature, and it can also help us with the perennially unpopular SPaG. It's hard to deny that the teaching of grammar has a generally poor rep – but there is joy to be found in it! Approached in the right way, it can be just as interesting as teaching Caribbean poetry or the conventions of Gothic fiction. But there are better ways of doing it than teaching through mechanical and decontextualised exercises, which is what often tends to happen at KS2 and which is clearly putting children off the further study of English. Language teaching which neglects meaning and function in order to concentrate on terminology is not good language teaching. And literature teaching which ignores the detailed mechanics of language in order to concentrate only on meaning is not good literature teaching.

We envisage English teachers being at the heart of developing language awareness, not just in their classrooms but at school level. In Chapter 8, we map out some suggestions as to how this can be achieved. But before that, we turn to another area that, along with English, should be at the centre of the push for language awareness: Modern Foreign Languages.

Notes

1 London: Cassell (1998).
2 Crystal, D. (2017), *Making Sense: The Glamorous Story of English Grammar.* London: Profile Books.
3 Clayton, D. & McCallum, A. (2018), *KS3 Language Laboratory.* London: English and Media Centre.
4 Crystal, D. (2012), *Spell it Out: The Singular Story of English Spelling.* London: Profile Books.

Why should we teach Modern Foreign Languages?

6.1 Introduction: a thought before we start

Native speakers of English tend to react with a mixture of embarrassment and awe when faced with the English language competence of others. 'They speak English better than we do...' 'It puts us to shame...' 'Why don't we learn other languages the way they do...?'

It's worth considering for a moment, though, how that seemingly effortless English competence is actually achieved. Bilingual schools are a common approach. In the Netherlands, for example, since 1989 a network of bilingual secondary schools has existed where students can expect to be taught 50 per cent of subjects in English. Of course, the Netherlands is a wealthy and go-ahead kind of country, and the Dutch are famous for their ease with speaking English. But actually, bilingual schools can be found almost everywhere, and even especially in developing countries. From Peru (where the authors taught together in a bilingual school in Lima) to Pakistan and Papua New Guinea, and most points in between, education through the medium of English is extraordinarily highly valued. And wherever in the world you are, if you are not lucky or wealthy enough to be able to access such schools, there is the state school system, where English (of variable quality) is often taught from primary school level, and the ubiquitous 'English institute', offering tuition (of equally variable quality) to adults in the early mornings and evenings.

Then there is the relentless reinforcement of English in the form of movies, video games, music, social media and so on, and the not insignificant fact that, pretty much wherever you want to travel, unless you happen to speak the local language, you're going to need English to have a business meeting, ask directions, order a meal or book into a hotel. Oh – and the small matter that when you apply for any kind of non-manual job (and even some manual ones), one of the first questions you're likely to be asked is: 'Do you speak English?' In many countries, you can't even graduate from high school or university, in *any* subject, unless you have 'passed English'. That's a pretty strong motivation to learn the language. So the

DOI: 10.4324/9781003201281-8

next time you wonder why we don't 'do' languages better, it's worth asking yourself: is there any way in the UK (or Australia, or Ireland, or the US or wherever) that we could recreate this kind of language learning environment? Can we really imagine a scenario whereby we used another language for anything up to half the school day, and continued to encounter and engage with that language in the evenings, at weekends, at work and on holiday? Can we imagine putting that level of investment of money, time and effort into language learning?

And if we *could* hypothetically reproduce that scenario, then which language would it be? Which other language is of such obvious, immediate and universally applicable benefit to anyone who learns it? None of the other 'big' languages of the world, such as Spanish, Chinese, French, Arabic or Urdu-Hindi, with their hundreds of millions of speakers, attracts cross-national non-native speakers in anything close to the way English does. The Austrian linguist Barbara Seidlhofer puts it starkly: 'The global spread of English is unprecedented and unparalleled... No other language called "world language" has ever had both the global expansion and the penetration of social strata and domains of use that English now has.'[1]

The truth is that people in most countries probably aren't particularly 'good at languages' at all. They're just highly aware of the value of learning English, 'the world's second language', as it has rightly been called. Try to keep that thought in mind as we go on to consider the position of modern foreign languages (MFL) in the first English-speaking country of all.

6.2 The Cinderella subject (and how it's not going to the ball anytime soon)

Two men are in a pub. One says, 'I've taught my dog to speak French.' 'Really?' says his mate, 'Let's hear him, then.' 'I said I taught him', comes the reply. 'I didn't say he'd learnt it'.

Pretty much every UK-born adult over the age of about forty has had some years of instruction in French, with what are, by any international standards, up-to-date and expertly designed textbooks, well-trained and highly competent teachers, and excellent audiovisual facilities and resources. So if you were to venture into the streets of Swansea, say, or Leicester or Aberdeen, and inquire of passers-by *Excusez-moi, savez-vous où se trouve le marchand de journaux le plus proche?* how confident would you be of being quickly pointed in the direction of the nearest newsagent? Granted, you might possibly do better with something more easily guessable, like *la poste de police*, or more recognisable, like *la gare*, but still – you could well be waiting quite a while, couldn't you?

It might be something that gives you sleepless nights, or it might not (not everyone cares – see our discussion in Section 6.3 below): but it is demonstrably the case that most Brits cannot manage even a basic conversation in a foreign language, despite that substantial exposure at school. A European Commission survey in 2012 showed that just 9 per cent of 14 and 15 year-old pupils in England reached the level of being 'an independent language user who can deal with straightforward familiar matters' in their first foreign language.[2] And as this might suggest, languages are not popular school subjects. According to Ofqual, entries for MFL exams have halved since 2002 (when there were around half a million entries).[3] Given a choice, students appear to vote with their feet: after 2004, when MFLs became optional after age 14, the decline went from steady to precipitous. There have been slight recoveries here and there (some linked to changes in accountability regimes, some to things like the increased popularity of Spanish), but there has been no sign of a real recovery in the longer term. Every year after GCSE and A level results time, when the statistics are produced, the evidence is grim: modern languages continue to decline in popularity, and the decline has now spread even into the independent sector, where languages were once thought of as secure (and prestigious).

The present position was summed up by a recently qualified MFL teacher in a blog post hosted by the British Educational Research Association: 'The teaching of modern foreign languages in English secondary schools is generally accepted to be in crisis… Even teachers don't seem to be enjoying their subject: according to a survey by the popular app Teacher Tapp, teachers of MFL are the least likely to agree that "the topics I teach inspire me."'[4] Against this dire backdrop, though, there exists a constant hum of government and think-tank promotion of languages: we are routinely told that foreign languages must be started earlier, at primary school; that the economy urgently needs language skills; that we need more foreign languages, not fewer (see, for example, the Scottish government's 1 + 2 model, which we refer to briefly in the next chapter). Not least, we are assured with some regularity that the key to future economic success lies with learning Mandarin Chinese.

What on earth is going on with MFLs? What is the background to all this and how did we end up here? Can we use some insights from applied linguistics and sociolinguistics perhaps, in order to understand things better? In this pair of chapters we use our language awareness approach to try to clarify a number of myths and misconceptions, supply some frameworks to help explain the issues, and, if not exactly point a surefire way to a buzzing MFL sector, then at least suggest some ways in which things might eventually be stabilised. After all, we are both lovers of language and languages, and as language people, we want to see MFLs thrive. But this necessitates making some hard arguments.

We'll begin at the very beginning: by considering why we need to learn foreign languages at all.

6.3 Why study another language?

In the English-speaking nations, bewailing the state of foreign language teaching has become something of a mini-industry in its own right. Academics generate a steady stream of articles and conference papers about how the anglophone countries are experiencing a lack of interest in language learning, and fret earnestly about things like 'constructing English monolingualism in educational practice' and 'silencing of plurilingual competencies in anglophone classrooms'. But while MFL teachers and lecturers – who by definition are interested in languages, and think languages are important – talk a lot about the 'crisis' in language take-up, lots of people, to be perfectly honest, are indifferent. It really isn't self-evident to many that languages are of great importance. And one thing worth noting is that all this concern about children's failure to engage with languages is in fact a fairly recent phenomenon. As one former senior HMI explains in his historical overview of MFL teaching in England,[5] the widespread expectation that all pupils should have exposure to foreign languages dates from only a few decades ago. Before the advent of comprehensive schools, MFLs were largely restricted to grammar schools and the private sector, and very few of the 80 per cent of children who attended secondary modern schools studied them. Hence in 1977, for example, only 10 per cent of pupils overall took a language O or A level. For whatever reason, it's always tended to be something of a minority pursuit.

As we remarked in the introduction to this chapter, there's probably one big reason for that (alongside lots of other, smaller ones), and it's a reason that has been growing steadily in importance for decades now. For vast swathes of the world's population, the question of why you should learn another language, beyond the dominant language of the country or region where you live, is something of a no-brainer. And the question of which language to choose is similarly uncontroversial. Which language and why, in other words, are questions which only English speakers really need to answer – because for pretty much everyone else on earth, it is perfectly obvious that to do many things you're going to need to learn an 'extra' language (a 'language of wider communication' or LWC, as sociolinguists say), and that nine times out of ten, that language is going to be English. The British Council reckons that there might be around 1.5 billion English learners in the world: in China alone, estimates of the numbers learning English range from 250 million to a colossal 650 million, and relatively few people are studying any other language. In English-as-a-Second-Language countries like India or Nigeria or Malaysia, you're even going to need to learn English to speak to many of your own compatriots. Worldwide, for every one native speaker of English there are at least four or five users of the language who have learnt it as a second or foreign language. English really is the world's lingua franca, then, and those who already speak it therefore have no obvious, urgent need to learn something else, whether you like the idea or not.

And lots of people don't like it, of course. Foreign language advocates and MFL teachers in the UK often have very limited patience with this argument, regarding it as insular, lazy or even arrogant. Baroness Jean Coussins, for example, joint chair of the all-party parliamentary group on modern languages, was quoted in 2019 by the BBC as saying: 'We are complacent. In the 21st century, speaking only English is as much of a disadvantage as speaking no English at all.'[6] That is simply not the case, of course, as a few moments' logical thought about the role of English in the world will make abundantly clear. But we certainly don't wish to take a silly, jingoistic 'English is best' line here, as if to match the Baroness's silly (and lazy) claim about the supposed risks of English monolingualism. The serious point is that the global dominance of English is a sociolinguistic fact, and supporters of foreign language teaching therefore need to take it on board and address it seriously if they are to make persuasive arguments as to why English-speaking children should learn another language – which we are going to try to do later on in the chapter. Platitudes and airy assertions won't do.

And so it's really not good enough when, for example, Ian Bauckham, who chaired a 2016 Teaching Schools Council (TSC) review into MFL pedagogy, writes in the introduction to that review:

> As a teacher and a linguist, I know that there are powerful educational benefits and career and workplace advantages to be gained from studying a modern foreign language… It is also important that, as a country, the United Kingdom has a strong foreign language capacity.

OK – but why *exactly* is it so important for schools to teach other languages? What *exactly* are the advantages that children, and indeed the country, gain from it? What do they risk losing by not having it? We think it's worth digging down into this, and looking in a bit of detail at the most commonly cited reasons for learning another language at school. As will become clear in due course, we think that there is a very good case for the teaching and promotion of language learning (and we are ourselves speakers of other languages). But we also think that some of the more popular and familiar arguments for it are less than convincing – and we suspect that children and their parents have noticed this.

Surveying the literature online, it would seem that most of the arguments boil down essentially to variations on seven key themes. These are that learning a language:

1. enables us to communicate internationally

2. brings economic benefit to the country

3. brings economic benefit to the student

4. gives us access to another culture

5. makes us see the world in a different way

6. has cognitive/developmental benefits

7. increases knowledge about language and language learning

We'll discuss each of these reasons in turn, and see if they can help us towards a concrete, rational and substantive case for why we should be teaching MFLs.

6.3.1 Learning another language enables us to communicate internationally

We begin with this one because it is probably the reason that is most often given, and because it seems the most obvious. But it's not as transparent as it seems. The idea that the *primary* aim of language teaching is to facilitate international communication is actually a fairly recent one in many contexts. It only became settled in the approach of UK schools in the 1980s, in line with the consensus arrived at following the Council of Europe's project *Learning and Teaching Modern Languages for Communication*, carried out between 1981 and 1988, which established the fundamental aims and methods of MFL teaching to be followed across a swathe of European countries. Prior to this, it had generally been thought (or just vaguely assumed by default) that the main aim of MFL teaching was to broaden the mind, and to allow students to access 'Great Cultures', and especially literatures, directly (see Section 6.3.4 below) – which also helps explain why languages had not been considered essential for supposedly less academic secondary modern pupils. The new emphasis on communication as an aim was echoed in the seal of approval the project bestowed on 'communicative' language teaching, as opposed to so-called grammar-translation, as the primary methodological approach.

An early pioneer of the language awareness movement in the UK, Eric Hawkins, observed at the turn of the millennium that with hindsight it was probably a serious strategic mistake for British schools to go along with the consensus, much though it might have made sense for the other countries involved (with the possible exception of Ireland, of course).[7] It had the effect of positioning speaking another language as a useful skill for day-to-day living, rather than as an integral and natural part of a well-rounded education. One problem with this, Hawkins noted, was that it diverted students' and teachers' attention away from the wider value of language awareness, or knowledge about language, that is to be had from MFL study. While the pendulum now seems to have swung back again towards a renewed focus on how language and spelling systems work (see the changes to French, German and Spanish GCSE announced in 2022, with the first exams being taken in 2026), it might well be too little, too late.

The other problem with it is that, as we have already suggested, if you're an English speaker then as a motivation to learn another language, it doesn't really cut it. The weaknesses of the 'languages for communication' narrative are not hard to see. Until quite recently, the website of St John's University, based in the notably multilingual borough of Queens in New York City, promoted its MFL offering in these terms:

> In a world that is increasingly interdependent, we can no longer afford to remain monolingual. Success depends in large measure on the ability of an individual to function as a member of a global village whose members speak a variety of languages.

That sounds superficially convincing, but on careful examination it's not entirely clear how the second sentence coheres with the first. These assertions (for they are really no more than that) are followed up with this:

> Learning foreign languages is no longer a pastime: it is a necessity. In large metropolitan areas such as New York, knowing a foreign language seems almost an essential aspect of urban living.[8]

Again, this is a persuasive-sounding claim, but if you stop to look at it properly, you can see the difficulty: it's actually just *not true*, which is presumably why it suddenly vanished from the website. How on earth is it a 'necessity' or 'almost essential' to speak another language in New York (or London, or Sydney, or Toronto)? And once again – which language would you choose? In Queens, if we take a quick look at the latest US census figures, Korean would actually be pretty useful – but so would Spanish, of course, along with Haitian Creole, Russian, Tagalog, Greek and a score of others. According to that 2015 census, more than 56 per cent of the population of Queens speak a language other than English at home.[9] Widespread multilingualism is literally the reason, of course, why lingua francas develop – it's to save people from having to spend years learning lots of languages in order to be able to communicate with each other. It's why the countries of the ASEAN bloc (Thailand, Indonesia, Vietnam, Philippines etc.), for example, use English as their sole official language among themselves, even though back at home in their respective countries, pretty much nobody speaks it as a mother tongue. The existence of multilingualism is not, in itself, an argument for learning other languages.

To be fair, in the case of the United States you could argue that it might be a good idea (though still far from a necessity) to learn Spanish, simply because of the presence there of such large numbers of Spanish speakers and the increasing public use of the language. It's the undisputed number two language of the country, the language of its most populous neighbour, Mexico, and of maybe 400 million speakers in Latin America as a whole, right there in the 'backyard'. And it has more native speakers than English, into the bargain. But what should we learn here in the UK? Spanish here is not really the same thing, sociolinguistically speaking. In Europe we tend to associate Spanish primarily with Spain – and every European knows that you don't need much Spanish to go on holiday to Benidorm or Magaluf, or even to visit the Museo del Prado, if your holiday is a more high-minded affair. Even the two Spanish boys Steve talked to at his school cheerfully acknowledged that there was little point in their English classmates learning Spanish for strictly communicative reasons (though they argued that language learning did have other benefits). French has nothing like the international presence and utility it had, say, a century ago – and by the way, why then do we still insist on teaching people French as a first foreign language, given how off-putting to many its grammar and phonology have often proved to be? German? Great if you want to speak to native speakers, but of fairly limited use beyond that. Italian, Portuguese, one of the Scandinavian languages? Ditto. Chinese? Well, we'll discuss that particular case in detail in the next chapter.

The struggle to justify the investment of your time and effort is especially daunting when you consider what a slow process it is to learn another language to a decent standard, and the reputation languages have as hard subjects in which to get good GCSE and A level grades. A few years ago, 152 language academics from British universities wrote an open letter complaining that Ofqual was 'killing off' MFLs by allowing them to be disproportionately harshly graded compared to other subjects. They ended by asking, reasonably enough: 'Where's the incentive to choose a language if you're systematically made to feel rubbish at it?'[10]

In short: the immediate communicative value of English is perfectly plain to speakers of other languages. But the immediate communicative value of other MFLs to English speakers is just not that obvious, especially relative to their perceived difficulty. If the value *were* that obvious, pupils would be rushing to take them up, and their parents would be demanding more and better MFL teaching, in the way they do with English in other countries. MFL teachers would be breezily confident about the future of their subject.

But that's not where we are.

6.3.2 Languages bring economic benefit to the country

In 2019 the British Council posted an interview online with Professor Mike Kelly, a 'languages advocate, expert and advisor' to the all-party parliamentary group on modern languages, following the publication of the National Recovery Programme for Languages, which set strategic language objectives for schools, universities, businesses, government and society in general. Asked: 'What does the UK miss out on by relying on Anglophone export markets?', Professor Kelly replied: 'New areas of growth. For the UK to take full advantage of trade opportunities overseas, we need to be much more open to trading in other languages.' Perhaps sensing that this in itself didn't really prove his point, he gave examples of the kind of problems that monolingualism supposedly leads to:

> Initial inquiries can be misunderstood or go unanswered. Customer information like brochures and websites may only be available in English. Sales representatives cannot establish the kind of rapport that business arrangements require.[11]

He concluded, naturally enough, that this meant that British school students should be more interested in languages. Meanwhile, in another recent interview published online, the British Council's head of schools programmes remarked:

Languages matter to the UK's future prosperity. Businesses are crying out for people with language skills so we need far more of our young people to learn languages both to boost their own job prospects and to ensure that the UK stays competitive on the world stage.[12]

The kind of discourse represented in these examples is characteristic of the 'languages-for-business' argument as put by commercially-minded MFL advocates. It is a simple and potentially persuasive narrative: it holds that, because not enough young people are incentivised to learn languages, the UK misses out on huge trading opportunities that it could otherwise seize. The parliamentary group supplies a figure for the resultant losses, cited as a straightforward fact in the same interview: 'The UK loses 3.5 percent of GDP in lost business opportunities due to our poor language skills'.

Now, this 3.5 per cent is interesting. It has become a totemic figure, being wheeled out time and again, during any and all discussion of the UK's lack of language skills to justify increased emphasis on MFL provision at school (it pops up, for example, in the British Academy's 2020 report *Towards A National Languages Policy: Education and Skills*). It is not at all surprising or unreasonable, of course, for people who have a professional interest in MFL teaching and learning to advocate for more of it, and such a precise figure is striking. But when you look a little more closely into its provenance, you find that it is not the clinching argument for MFL teaching that it at first appears.

The figure comes from as far back as 2014, and a report by economists James Foreman-Peck and Yi Wang of Cardiff Business School, commissioned by a now-defunct government department called UK Trade and Investment. It was called *The Costs to the UK of Language Deficiencies as a Barrier to UK Engagement in Exporting*. If you actually read this report – which rather few people appear to have done – something very interesting emerges. Yes, the authors do put forward the 3.5 per cent figure, and yes, they do indeed argue that UK business requires enhanced language skills in order to trade further and wider than English-using markets. However – and it's a very big however – they do not argue that more people should therefore be encouraged to take up languages at school. In fact, the report quite explicitly recommends that where firms encounter problems of language or culture in engaging with overseas markets, they should respond by employing native speakers of the languages concerned. Helpfully, Foreman-Peck and Wang point out that there are overseas students studying for MBAs and similar qualifications in university towns and cities all over the UK who can be hired or offered internships.

Let us be clear, then: while arguing that the UK needs foreign language and cross-cultural skills, the authors of that report do *not* think that the best response to this is to put large-scale investment into teaching languages at school. And nor would you expect hard-headed economists to recommend that, when you think about it. It makes little sense to teach large numbers of schoolchildren or university students Chinese, for example, given how challenging Chinese typically is for English speakers, when it would be vastly cheaper, easier and more effective to hire a Chinese MBA student to help with contacts and cultural understanding.

And again – yes, we know it's beginning to get repetitive! – if you *were* to decide large-scale investment in language teaching was the way forward, the same old question remains. Which language would you choose to invest in, when you already speak the most widespread trading language that has ever existed on earth, and when it is entirely unclear which other one will be of most commercial benefit at an unspecified point in the future? This goes not just for the business concerned or for the country as a whole, but for the individual students themselves, too.

Let's take a look at that question.

6.3.3 Learning languages brings economic benefit to the student

This argument, even more than the last one, rests first and foremost on the question of which language you choose to learn – in fact, it is entirely inseparable from it. No language will ever bring the learner the kind of guaranteed return (in so far as such things can ever really be guaranteed) that English promises. A Swiss specialist in language economics, François Grin, has calculated that learning English to a very good standard in Switzerland could yield an earnings differential in employment of around 25 per cent.[13] Now, even with all the caveats and variables that Professor Grin adduces, that's still a pretty good investment, all things considered. But even for the case of English, as he goes on to note, the return depends very much on what else you choose to learn alongside it. Trade and commerce-oriented subjects do very well: others do not. So if you study, say, English and International Business at university, you'll be well placed to see some of that lovely earnings boost – but if you choose English and Education Studies, it's much, much less likely.

For us here in the UK, the lessons are unmistakable. If you're absolutely convinced from an early age that your adult future lies in selling goods into French-speaking markets, then choosing to learn French is a rock-solid investment in that future. But how many people, realistically, are sure at the age of eleven or even earlier not only about what they are going to do in the future, but about where they are likely to end up doing it? The economic benefit of learning another, random language is likely to be negligible – or at least, no greater than the benefit of studying drama, or music, or any other of the humanities. And what economists call the 'opportunity cost' is therefore much higher for an English speaker learning French or Chinese, say, than it is for a French or Chinese speaker learning English. That is to say, if your motivation to learn a language is primarily economic, you might well be – all things considered, and in the long run – actually better off learning something else.

6.3.4 Learning another language gives us access to another culture

During a discussion about languages at school on the *Mumsnet* website, one rather grumpy contributor commented:

> We waste far too much money on a curriculum that is useless for your average citizen who has little interest in other cultures.

Now, you might argue that this is exactly why you *should* teach languages – in order to develop the child's interest in cultures other than their own. In the past, as we noted earlier, a large part of the reason for teaching languages was to facilitate access to a 'great' culture: first Latin and Ancient Greek, and later, most notably, French (and to some extent, German). This complacently Eurocentric view of language and culture hasn't aged very well, and doesn't sit comfortably with some modern societal attitudes – though as we will argue in the next chapter, the traces of it are still very visible. (Why are e.g. French and German regarded as modern foreign languages, but Tamil or Bengali as 'community' languages?)

While some MFL teachers have a strong interest in language, and identify and position primarily themselves as linguists (in the sense of a specialist in language and how it works), probably the majority are more comfortable in the role of informal cultural ambassador and enthusiast for the French language and all things French, the Spanish language and all things Hispanic, or whatever it may be. It's a divide which to some extent mirrors the divide in English departments between the literature specialists and the language people. Quiz a UK-born language teacher and it's a fair bet that you'll find somewhere in their past a fantastic school exchange, a life-changing year abroad or a fondly-remembered family holiday in a certain country. It goes without saying that this kind of interest and enthusiasm for the subject can be highly motivating for students. But if a pupil has little interest in, say, French culture, and doesn't intend to visit a francophone country anytime soon (the language-for-communication rationale that we discussed just now) then this leaves little to attract them to a national culture-oriented MFL classroom. Note, of course, that a lack of interest in one particular national or linguistic culture doesn't at all necessarily imply a lack of interest in any of them. We have met quite a lot of young people who are resolutely indifferent to mainstream European culture, for example, but who are utterly transfixed by all things Korean, or Japanese.

So language teaching absolutely needs cultural context, and one of the key benefits of language learning is the opportunity it offers to understand how social practice and social interaction can vary from one country and language to another. But the wider, more enduring and universal value to the learner lies not so much in specific cultural knowledge itself, which is necessarily limited and can be superficial or stereotypical (the Spanish dine late, the Dutch are straightforward, the Germans aren't keen on small talk) but in *intercultural* knowledge, as the academic jargon has it. Acquiring intercultural awareness means acquiring critical insight into your own society, your own language, your own way of seeing the world, through exploring that of others. That is to say: children understand themselves and their own culture better when they are required to engage with another culture, whichever it may be. It's doubtful that Rudyard Kipling ever uttered the word 'interculturality' in his life, but that's partly what he was getting at when he lamented, 'What do they know of England, who only England know?'

Potentially, then, in the hands of a skilled teacher who is attuned to this kind of thinking, learning *any* language can be rewarding for schoolchildren, as it aids personal development and understanding of how we perceive ourselves and our culture, and how we are in turn perceived by others. Developing in children the critical insight afforded by interculturality is therefore a much more durable outcome of learning a language than a surface familiarity with 'how foreigners do things'. It has been remarked that as human beings, we don't notice the culture that surrounds us as we grow up, any more than a fish notices the water in which it swims. Language teaching with an intercultural edge makes learners *notice* – for example, through comparing systematically the home language/culture and the target language/culture, and inviting them to reflect critically on the similarities and differences.

And this links straight to our next reason for learning languages.

6.3.5 Learning another language makes us see the world in a different way

This and the previous discussion about interculturality are in a sense two sides of the same coin. They're both to do with being jolted out of cultural inertia, as it were, or being taken out of your comfort zone. To encounter a different language at school is often a young person's first taste of real 'otherness', of the realisation that their way of saying and naming things is not the only one, or necessarily the most natural or logical one. Other languages have different word orders (e.g. German), different tense/aspect systems (e.g. French), they classify and divide the world up in subtly different ways.

So to learn to speak another language is to begin to see the world through someone else's eyes, and even more so if the language in question is an ancient or non-European one, or is written using an unfamiliar (or even non-alphabetic) script. I (Tim) once did a small piece of language attitudes research at a secondary school in Sheffield which offered a 'carousel' experience in the first year, so that each student had a short taster course of French, German and Urdu before choosing which language they would like to opt for. Now, the interesting thing about the results was that not a single non-Asian student went on to study Urdu – *but* virtually every one of them did report increased interest in the cultural background of their Urdu-speaking classmates, and dramatically more positive attitudes towards Urdu as a language. That's actually not a bad result. In fact, while a 'language learning experience' of that kind is guaranteed to enthuse and hone the ideas of children who are already interested in languages and intend to pursue them seriously, it can also do a lot to broaden the horizons even of those children who will not go on to study languages in great depth. That is to say, it broadens your horizons even if you never advance very far: the psychological work has been done.

Given how hard it is for the average English speaker to reach a good level of competence in Chinese – basic literacy in that language is usually considered to consist of the memorisation of two to three thousand characters, as we will see in the next chapter – it is probably this mind-opening, awareness-raising experience, rather than any great communicative benefit, that is the main value of learning Chinese. It was probably the main value of learning Japanese, too, when that was briefly a thing, back in the 1990s. As we have already suggested, the economic benefits of language learning are intangible at best if you're an English speaker. But the benefits in terms of personal development are enormous: people who have had exposure to other ways of saying, other ways of interpreting reality, really do tend to have a more rounded and nuanced view of the way the world works. By the same token, someone who has never tried to navigate a foreign language necessarily has a restricted understanding of the extraordinary variety of humankind, even if they don't realise it. As Prof Richard Johnstone has remarked, 'a life lived monolingually misses out on something that is essentially human'.[14]

Fortunately, in the words of a bumper sticker slogan I once saw on a Los Angeles freeway, 'monolingualism is curable'.

6.3.6 Language learning has cognitive benefits for the student

The mind-opening effect is in fact thought by many to go even further than this. It has long been recognised that children brought up bilingually or multilingually often seem to have a cognitive advantage over their monolingual peers. A large-scale study for the British Academy by Professors Bencie Woll and Li Wei[15] extended this idea by focusing on the cognitive benefits of actual language learning. They concluded that, among other things, learning another language (including a sign language, of course) improved attention and mental alertness, had a positive cross-curricular effect on attainment in English, literacy, maths and science, and enhanced creative flexibility, originality, resourcefulness and social empathy.

One member of a focus group established during the study, a PGCE tutor, remarked that: 'Many families face challenges in their everyday lives and they find it hard to accept that learning a foreign language can help to improve their situation'. That sounds about right. Economically struggling, marginalised and underprivileged families are hardly likely to be persuaded that learning French should be an educational priority, if the benefits that it offers appear elusive, irrelevant or disproportionate to the effort involved. 'You will be able to speak to French people if you ever go to France' is not going to clinch the deal. But the British Academy study actually notes that the public are *not*, in general, resistant to the idea of learning languages. They are willing to be persuaded, at the very least – but they need to be persuaded with arguments that actually work and are relevant to them. The 'cross-curricular benefits' argument, then, is perhaps the kind of thing that MFL teachers and advocates need to be putting across, rather than focusing on the 'utility' or 'language-for-communication' arguments. These, as we have already argued, are likely to be viewed with a degree of deserved scepticism by many children and their parents.

Might a concerted attempt to emphasise the cognitive and intellectual benefits of language learning start to shift opinions? It just might. Of course, other subjects have developmental and intellectual benefits too; and, of course, there is only so much space in the curriculum. But few other subjects have such a positive cognitive effect as languages, at so many different levels.

And there's one more guaranteed, life-long benefit, too.

6.3.7 Language learning develops knowledge about language and about language learning itself

We noted at Section 6.3.3 above that it's impossible to predict with any accuracy which language(s) an English-speaking child at the age of eleven is likely to want or need to know in the future. And therefore logically, as the TSC review of MFL pedagogy put it, 'it is important that language teaching gives them explicit language knowledge and strategies which can help them with future study of other languages'. As language enthusiasts ourselves (and both relative latecomers to our main second language, Spanish), we think that's absolutely the case. We therefore welcome the current emphasis on the crunchy, language-y bits of language learning, instead of just 'communication' – which, as we noted above, many children and their parents never quite bought, and couldn't quite see the point of. The current subject content document for MFL, published in 2015, states that GCSE specifications should enable students to 'deepen their knowledge about how language works and enrich their vocabulary'; and the chair of the TSC review has written that 'we state unequivocally that vocabulary, grammar and phonics constitute the substantive, first-order knowledge base we need to master if our pupils are to say they "know" the language'.

But, encouraging as this is, it doesn't yet go far enough. It is the 'knowledge about how language works' that is really the key here, and the ominous focus on 'vocabulary, grammar and phonics' seems to be starting to row back from it, bringing echoes of the reductive discourses around English which we discussed in some detail in Chapters 3 and 4. When a child starts the study of another language, they begin the process of learning how to learn languages (and learning what works for them, and what doesn't). Language-aware teachers will be constantly drawing learners' attention to things: comparing with the native language, pointing out cognates and memorable etymologies, sharing vocabulary-building tips, exemplifying and explaining pronunciation, distinguishing the vital aspects of the new language from the moderately useful. A French or a Spanish or a German classroom is first and foremost a *language* classroom.

Inescapably, this means that MFL teachers really should have a basic grounding in linguistics. They don't need a PhD in Chomskyan syntactic theory, but they do need, among other things, a good understanding of how different grammar systems function, a smattering of semantics, an understanding of pragmatics (how language works in social context), a decent foundation in sociolinguistics (who in the world speaks Spanish/French/Chinese etc. in what circumstances, and why), and, not least, a decent grasp of phonetics and phonology. Here's a small example of why the last is so important. I (Tim) always liked language and languages at school, and did well enough in them to go on to read modern languages and linguistics at university. I thought I spoke pretty decent French – but it was only upon being introduced to linguistics in my first year at university that I found out about some of the technical differences between English and French, the ones that make the sounds of the two languages so characteristic.

There was the difference between the alveolar /d/ of English and the dental /d/ (the voiced dental plosive [d̪]) of French. Pronounce the /d/ sounds of *dedans* with your tongue against your top teeth instead of against your alveolar ridge, and your lips are naturally pushed outwards in a semi-pout. You really begin to *sound* French. Or there's the question of the syllable-timed rhythm of French as opposed to the stress-timing of English, so that in French each syllable gets pretty much the same stress. Say *Nicolas Sarkozy* with the stress on the *Ni-* and *-ko-* syllables, and you sound like a BBC newsreader, even if your pronunciation is otherwise perfect. Say it with approximately equal stress on each syllable (including the very last one) and you start to sound more like a French newsreader. In all my years of learning French at school, with truly outstanding, formidably well-qualified teachers, not one of those teachers had ever pointed these things out to me. Doubtless they had modelled them, because their spoken French was excellent, but they had not explicitly explained them. Why not? Very probably because they were not consciously aware of them, because their own decades-long experience of the study of French language and literature had never included the vital elements of phonetics and phonology.

Phonetics and phonology show us how sounds are made and how the sound systems of different languages function differently. This huge insight is full of intercultural awareness promise – it guides us towards an understanding of why Chinese speakers, for example, so often mix /l/ and /r/, why Spanish speakers sometimes have difficulty spelling words with *b* or *v* correctly, and so on. And, of course, the discipline of linguistics offers fresh insights into *all* areas of language learning, not just this one. This is why we hold out such high hopes for things like the Linguistics in MFL Project,[16] an initiative developed by a group of English universities explicitly to 'address the crisis in MFL uptake in schools', as they say on their website, by introducing school students to the subject of linguistics, through workshops, teacher professional development sessions and online resources. And then there's LASER, and the Linguistics Olympiad and other similar projects. A 2021 research article on the *Modern Languages Open* website[17] demonstrated that even a short introduction to linguistics was highly beneficial to students doing A Level MFL subjects. The students reported that they found the topics inherently interesting (they were language students, after all!) and that their confidence in their language skills was boosted. The authors also pointed out that the introduction of linguistics as a topic of study at school could go a long way to combatting 'Standard English only' and other harmful, prescriptive ideologies of the kind that we discussed in the first three chapters of this book. Is a new focus on linguistics a possible way out of the morass in which MFL has found itself? We'd like to think it can help, at the very least: whatever language you study, the underlying subject of study is language itself.

Two other important things, finally. Firstly, the sensitivity to language which is nurtured and developed in a language-oriented MFL classroom is something that can be of real and immediate use to anyone, even if they never feel the need to speak another language. Specifically, it might help native speakers of English to be better able to speak the kind of English that is favoured in mixed international contexts, where English is used as the lingua franca. (Notoriously, non-native speakers of English in such contexts often complain that it is the native speakers that they have difficulty understanding, not their fellow second language users.) So a teacher might point out, for example, the importance in cross-cultural encounters of speaking clearly, choosing simple grammatical forms, avoiding slang and regionalisms, monitoring constantly for understanding, and flexibly using a range of communicative strategies. The fact that English is the world's lingua franca does not mean that native speakers get a free pass: it means that they have particular communicative responsibilities to acknowledge.

Secondly, it is worth emphasising once more that a good language learning experience in the hands of a skilled teacher doesn't just provide children with strategies for future language learning. It also engenders (just as importantly) a positive *attitude* towards languages and language learning. It might even, as in the Urdu case above, give students positive attitudes towards the 'target language community', as the applied linguistics jargon has it. In any case, it is a solid argument for the importance of MFL provision in schools, as long as it is taught and presented in a way that makes the benefits clear to the learner.

6.4 Conclusion

Both of us, the authors, had transformative experiences in MFL classes at school, which led us to a lifelong interest in and enthusiasm for languages. We didn't know the phrase back then, but what we had picked up was some degree of language awareness. And the language awareness pioneer Eric Hawkins, whom we referred to in Section 6.3.1 above, was surely right: in the context of English-speaking countries, language awareness, in its broadest sense, is probably the best reason of all for choosing to teach and learn languages. MFLs are a fundamental part of a good education, but teachers need to be clear in their own minds about the reasons for learning them, so they can motivate pupils better, and convince pupils and their parents of the real-world benefits that language study brings.

Good language teaching goes far, far beyond vocabulary-building and pronunciation. It helps personal and social development through intercultural tasks and activities; it provides a training in how to learn languages, and even in how to use one's mother tongue more effectively; it provides cross-curricular enhancement and development of communication and social skills; it opens the mind to new ways of seeing the world; and it does all this as part of that 'rounded education' that we mentioned at the beginning of the chapter. In emphasising the cognitive, intercultural and developmental benefits of language learning, while developing a systematic focus on how language works, we begin to show pupils and their parents what language study can do for them, now and throughout their lives. This is where MFL teaching and learning from a language awareness perspective leads us.

Notes

1 Seidlhofer, B. (2011), *Understanding English as a Lingua Franca*. Oxford: Oxford University Press, p. 3.
2 European Commission (2012), *First European Survey of Language Competences. Final Report*.
3 Churchward, D. (2019), *Recent Trends in Modern Foreign Language Exam Entries in Anglophone Countries*. Coventry: Ofqual.
4 https://www.bera.ac.uk/blog/content-and-language-integrated-learning-and-extensive-processing-instruction-a-useful-partnership-for-language-teaching
5 Dobson, A. (2018), 'Towards "MFL for all" in England: a historical perspective'. *The Language Learning Journal* 46: 71–85.
6 https://www.bbc.com/news/education-47421735
7 Hawkins, E. (1999), 'Foreign language study and Language Awareness'. *Language Awareness* 8 (3/4): 124–42.
8 English, F. & Marr, T. (2015), *Why Do Linguistics?* London & New York: Bloomsbury, p. 222.
9 https://www.babbel.com/en/magazine/the-languages-of-queens-diversity-capital-of-the-world
10 *The Guardian*, 11 May 2019.
11 https://www.britishcouncil.org/voices-magazine/uk-language-learning-crisis
12 https://www.teachsecondary.com/english-and-mfl/view/give-teens-a-reason-to-study-a-language
13 Grin, F. (2003), 'Language planning and economics'. *Current Issues in Language Planning* 4 (1): 1–66.
14 In Lo Bianco, J. & Slaughter, Y. (2009), *Second Languages and Australian Schooling*. Camberwell: Australian Council for Educational Research.
15 Woll, B. & Li Wei (2019), 'Cognitive benefits of language learning: broadening our perspectives'. Final Report to the British Academy. https://www.thebritishacademy.ac.uk/projects/cognitive-benefits-language-learning/
16 https://linguisticsinmfl.co.uk/
17 Sheehan, M., Corr, A., Havinga, A., Kasstan, J. & Schifano, N. (2021), 'Rethinking the UK languages curriculum: arguments for the inclusion of linguistics'. *Modern Languages Open* 1: 14. DOI: 10.3828/mlo.v0i0.368

7 Which MFL? And is earlier really better?

7.1 Introduction

When it comes to deciding which language to study or offer, and at what stage of a child's school career this should begin to happen, there is a vast amount of information, advice and opinion out there. While it varies in quality, there are common themes. Certain languages, for example, are deemed to offer more of a concrete benefit than others, as we mentioned in the last chapter: 'Chinese proficiency creates countless economic opportunities', claims one language teaching company. Meanwhile, the 'common sense' belief that the earlier children start learning a language, the better, is extraordinarily widespread – a fact that has not escaped commercial language teaching providers, like the private tuition company whose website asks 'WHEN SHOULD MY CHILD START LEARNING A LANGUAGE?' and immediately answers its own question: 'It is important to start as early as possible.' But why, exactly? The website text explains:

> A child who begins learning their second language at the age of 3 or 4 can speak like a native, which is a remarkable advantage. For an adult, this would entail a lot of hard work, but children do not think about languages in the same way.[1]

But is it really as simple as that?

Clearly, schools, pupils and parents have to make some difficult decisions – decisions with potentially quite serious, far-reaching consequences – in an area which abounds in myths and preconceptions, not to mention vested interests. So which language(s) should a school choose to offer? How should 'early' language learning be approached, and what scale of resources should be devoted to it? On what grounds should these decisions be made, and with reference to what information? We are going to use the insights of applied linguistics and sociolinguistics to attempt to work through these questions from a language-aware viewpoint.

DOI: 10.4324/9781003201281-9

7.2 Choosing a language

As we noted in the last chapter, the sociolinguistic evidence suggests that it is probably unhelpful to try to promote MFLs as being useful primarily for communication with the rest of the world, or for the direct economic benefit of the individual or the country. English-speaking students and parents alike are apt to consider these arguments, weigh them against the evidence of their own senses and life experience, and conclude that they are being sold a pup. A more persuasive argument is that having at least some degree of competence in another language is an integral part of a well-rounded education, and offers cognitive and cultural benefits which are real, if hard to define with precision (Joseph Lo Bianco's 2009 report for Australia suggests that this message is being picked up strongly in other English-speaking countries, too).[2]

But when it comes to the question of deciding which language(s) a school should offer, or which language a student should opt for, it becomes clear that there are competing and sometimes contradictory narratives in play, often couched in terms of prestige and/or usefulness, and one of which is certainly that of economic advancement. We're going to look now at some of the arguments attaching to the more commonly taught foreign languages in British schools, and see if we can establish some ground rules for choosing the language that is the best 'fit' for the future of any given child and the strategic objectives of the school.

7.2.1 The 'traditional' languages

The British Council's 2017 report *Languages for the Future* listed (in this order) Spanish, Mandarin, French, Arabic and German as the languages most likely to be useful for the UK's future prosperity and security; and these, basically, are the MFLs that schools will find most encouragement to offer. (The next five, out of interest, were Italian, Dutch, Portuguese, Japanese and Russian.) The same report tells us that French and German are in decline in UK schools, while Spanish is on a fairly steady rise, though starting from a low base, and Arabic and Mandarin are also growing, though starting from a *very* low base. We'll begin by briefly assessing the positions of the MFLs most familiar to most people, the ones that make up 90 percent of all pupils studying MFLs, and which teacher training courses focus on almost exclusively: French, Spanish and German.

Doing French at school is such a familiar part of most people's mental furniture that it is easy to forget why, exactly, it has been the default choice of MFL for so long. One recent post on the question-and-answer website Quora put the question in a cheerfully brutal manner: 'Why is French taught as a compulsory language in UK schools when few pupils have the remotest interest in learning it?' And indeed, if you ask school children in the 'compulsory' stage of language learning why it is French they are studying, you are likely to get some pretty vague answers, the most common being something along the lines that it is the language of our closest continental neighbour.

But geographical proximity has little to do with it, really – French has tradition-ally been learned as a second language in very many countries, even where there are no French-speaking communities nearby, simply because of its historical inter-national utility and accumulated weight of cultural prestige. For centuries, before its position was usurped by English, French was the acknowledged language of international diplomacy and politics, and the lingua franca of educated people in great swathes of the world. It is quite hard to imagine now just how dominant and influential French political thought, literature, science and language were, for a very long time; but while French has lost much of its global lingua franca role to English (though it is still indispensable in, for example, parts of Europe and north and west Africa and is an official language of the UN), the residual prestige remains. Significantly, so does much of the apparatus of teaching and learning. It was a compulsory and highly visible subject in grammar schools from age 11 right through to 16, and the custom of teaching it continued through the transition into the comprehensive era. The actual utility of the language is now perhaps second-ary as a reason for teaching it to the easy availability of teachers and materials.

It still stands, though, as an utterly solid language choice. Against this, the strongly middle-class and even elitist associations of French, derived directly from its grammar school history, can be a turn-off for some pupils (and perhaps espe-cially working-class boys, anecdotally); but, of course, there are ways of addressing this head-on. It's something of a cliché, but materials which feature internation-ally-known French-speaking sports people, musicians and suchlike, and reflect the multicultural reality of much of modern, urban France, can help establish rel-evance and interest. Back in the early 2000s, the mere existence of people like Arsenal footballers Thierry Henry and Patrick Vieira made the professional life of a friend of ours, a French teacher in an east London comprehensive, easier than it had ever previously been, as inner city boys discovered cool, black French speakers to emulate.

Perhaps more challenging to deal with is the perceived difficulty of the language for many English speakers. In its writing system (which only partially reflects the spoken language), in its sometimes baroque grammar, and in its phonology (those nasal vowels, that syllable timing!), French really can present formidable obsta-cles, causing learners to lose heart. For many adults, French was their first taste of learning a foreign language, and was unfortunately the one which put them off languages for life. French teachers who are language-aware tend to make a point of teaching *about* French, and hence about things like the speaking/writing distinc-tion, as well as teaching how to communicate in it or how to manage its grammar.

German? There is a 'Great Culture' history underlying German teaching, as with French, but no one seriously expects most modern-day 15-year-olds to be diving enthusiastically into Goethe and Thomas Mann. Rather, the predominant narrative around German is one of businesses needing German language skills and being willing to pay a premium for them. The British Council report we referred to earlier quotes the Finance Editor of *Business Insider* website: 'Speaking German will not only get you, in general, the highest-paid job, it is also the language that is in highest demand across job postings.' However, the same report acknowledges that only 8,000 or so jobs actually demanded a knowledge of German in 2017 (10,000 demanded French, and 4,000 Spanish, for the sake of comparison), and doesn't actually manage to say whether this was 8,000 jobs available at that moment in time, available every year, or what. Nor, crucially, does it tell us what level of competence was demanded. Will a GCSE grade 5 in German put a premium on your eventual salary, or does it need an honours degree? In fact, it is frustratingly difficult to get your hands on real, unvarnished data on the supposed benefits of German (or indeed, any other language, as we saw in the last chapter).

The fact that take-up of Spanish is on a rising trend might be linked to the enduring popularity of Spain as a tourist destination, and therefore to a certain familiarity with at least the look and sound of the language. It might more convincingly be seen, though, as a development in line with the general influence of American cultural trends in the rest of the world, and especially the western and western-oriented parts of it. As we noted in the previous chapter, Spanish has grown in visibility in the US to a quite extraordinary degree. The US is comfortably in the top five of countries with the most Spanish speakers, and depending on how the statistics are collected and terms defined, could even be in the top three (after Mexico and Colombia). Generations that grew up with bilingual, dual-heritage identity as something normal and unremarkable have now produced not just a big and self-confident Latino middle class, but instantly recognisable political figures, business people, public intellectuals, musicians, actors and sports stars. This all has a knock-on effect well beyond the borders of the United States.

One point to note, though. Spanish, like Mandarin, is sometimes marketed as being useful because of its numbers of speakers – even being positioned as a 'global' language, alongside English. But what makes a language a truly global one is not the number of native speakers it has, but the number of non-native speakers and their social and geographical spread. Proportionate to their vast numbers of native speakers (both exceeding the number of native speakers of English), Mandarin Chinese and Spanish are actually rather puny global players. A huge majority of Chinese speakers live in China itself or traditionally Chinese-speaking parts of the world, and well over 90 percent of Spanish speakers live in the Americas. Relatively speaking, rather few people worldwide learn Chinese or Spanish as a useful lingua franca, in the way that they might learn English or French.

So what about the case of Chinese, then? (Or Mandarin – there are technical linguistic issues around how these names are used, but we'll accept them here as interchangeable in line with most ordinary, non-specialist practice.) It's very much the 'new kid on the block' of the standard MFL offer, and it's probably the language which has the most assumptions, vague suggestions and preconceptions swirling around it.

7.2.2 Chinese: the language of the future?

When you start to look at the claims made for Chinese – by advocates for the language, by the schools that teach it, by companies offering Chinese language training in China or overseas – what strikes you first is their extraordinary boldness and confidence. In the nature and scale of what Chinese appears to promise to learners, it almost rivals the discourses associated with globally dominant English, with the added suggestion that Chinese is the *coming* language. The second noteworthy thing is that the same two notes are struck again and again: Chinese will give you an edge in the jobs market, and Chinese will develop your intellectual capabilities.

The Keats language school in China, for one, doesn't mince its words. For the career advantages of Mandarin:

> With Mandarin being needed in business, knowing the language will make you an attractive employee. If you know Mandarin, the company you're applying for will see you as a valuable person.

And as for the cognitive benefits:

> Did you know that learning Chinese utilizes areas of the brain that other languages do not? Studies have been done on this, which means learning Chinese takes intensive brainpower [...] English speakers use the left temporal lobe. Mandarin speakers use both![3]

The Ninchanese language learning app, in its enthusiasm, throws all caution to the winds:

> [T]he Mandarin Chinese language is a miracle tool to make the brain do its work. The Chinese language helps to activate a specific zone in your brain that other languages do not.

Another provider of education in Chinese, China Admissions, makes the point in scarcely less excitable terms:

> Learning Chinese makes you smart [...] Learning Chinese makes you smarter according to science. Researchers found that learning Chinese exercises your brain more than any other language.[4]

This 'miracle tool' and 'according to science' stuff is all faintly ludicrous, of course, and it's easy enough to knock down with a modicum of linguistic awareness. It does appear that Chinese speakers use the right side of the brain – which is associated with intonation and melody – as well as the left, to help them decode and interpret the sounds of Chinese. This is because in so-called tonal languages, differences in spoken pitch can change the meanings of words. But as several com-mentators pointed out when the research pertaining to this was first published in the early 2000s, you could argue that this makes Chinese much more difficult and tiring to process for an English speaker than a European language: there are no grounds at all for suggesting that using both hemispheres to understand Chinese 'makes you smarter'. It should also be noted that this is simply a characteristic of tonal languages in general, not Chinese in particular – if you really feel you must give your right hemisphere a linguistic work-out, you would do just as well with Thai or Vietnamese, say, or Igbo or Yoruba.

A moderate amount of sociolinguistic awareness will similarly help when we are faced with breezy, unsubstantiated claims about the supposed advantage that the learner of Chinese will gain in their career. As we pointed out in the last chap-ter, with the help of the Swiss professor, it is very hard indeed to attach any specific monetary advantage to knowing any particular language – even global English. And in any case, the idea that Chinese is 'needed in business' is a gigantic over-simpli-fication. It is based on one single, widespread but highly dubious notion: that a country's economic and political clout has a direct and proportional relationship to the perceived importance of its language.

As the historian of language Nicholas Ostler explains in his book *Empires of the Word: A Language History of the World* (HarperCollins, 2005), while this has sometimes been the case, equally often it turns out not to be. For example, Greek (in the Middle East) and Portuguese (in Asia) had historical importance as regional trading languages for centuries after Greece and Portugal had declined into near-irrelevance on the world stage. Meanwhile, the wealth of the countries of the Arabian Gulf has never once looked like translating into a global appetite for learning Arabic. The economic success of east Asian economies like those of Japan and Korea has gone hand-in-hand with some undeniable cultural visibility, such as the popularity of anime among young people in the US and Europe, and of K-Pop in Latin America and elsewhere; but there has been virtually zero added take-up of the languages. The worldwide spread of French and English in the nineteenth century had as much to do with French and British colonial expansion as with eco-nomic power or market share per se. The military and political dominance of the UK and then the US in the twentieth century, when coupled with the extraordinary reach of their shared language, have perhaps lured us into the careless assumption that this is how it always works. But it isn't: while there are certainly trends and tendencies, there is no sociolinguistic law that connects economic success auto-matically with language spread.

To our point, then. You wouldn't think that such unsophisticated puffery by advocates for Chinese would be terribly persuasive, when you're taking a decision as potentially important and far-reaching as choosing which language to special-ise in – but the narratives around Chinese sometimes seem to be accepted rather uncritically. In 2017, a bilingual prep school opened in London offering, for a cool £19,680 a year (in the school year 2022–23), a dual curriculum taught half in English and half in Mandarin. You'd expect some *very* hard facts to justify a figure like that. But the school's website,[5] in setting out its stall ('There are many reasons why Chinese is an important language to learn'), actually sells the supposed benefits of learning Chinese in terms hardly more sophisticated or precise than the Keats School or China Admissions managed. There are the usual lazy assumptions that a large number of speakers makes a language 'widely spoken' (even though these speakers are overwhelmingly concentrated in a single nation), and that a single big national economy automatically lends influence to a language:

It is the most widely spoken [language] on earth and is becoming increasingly influential thanks to China's ever growing economic, political and cultural power.

There is the unsubstantiated assertion that it will provide an automatic advantage in the jobs market:

Learning Chinese will improve a pupil's career opportunities. Knowing the language will give him/her an extra edge in the increasingly global economy.

And just to cap things off, there is the now-familiar trope about using both sides of the brain being a somehow beneficial exercise:

The learning of Chinese is an excellent opportunity to help children gain cognitive benefits. This is because, unlike most other languages, Chinese stimulates and activates the development of both sides of the brain (Welcome [*sic*] Trust UK, 2003).

In 2020 the *New Statesman*, reporting on the school, noted that pinned to the wall of the school's waiting room was a quote from Sir Martin Sorrell, businessman and founder of WPP plc, the world's largest advertising and PR group: 'Chinese and computer code are the only two languages the next generation should need.' This is so bizarrely reductive that you would be tempted to think it a joke, were it not for the deadly seriousness of everything else about the school.

For those not lucky enough to be able to afford £19,680 a year for an immersive experience, and therefore taking Chinese in the same way as French, i.e. as a normal school subject, there's also the question of level of competence. And this is the crucial question, really. Just how good would your Chinese have to be for it to bring you any real, tangible benefit? For example, how long would you have to study the language for, in order to be able to read a commercial briefing easily and discuss it with native speakers in a business meeting? Bear in mind at this point that you need to have memorised, say, 2,500–3,000 characters in order to have basic functional literacy. If you managed three new characters in every single class (which is actually a *very* big ask!), and you had three classes a week, every week of the school year, you're looking at maybe eight or nine years' worth of unbroken study, just to be able to read a newspaper. There's a good reason why the Chinese government puts such emphasis on English – they are not labouring under the illusion that most of the rest of the world is ever going to learn enough Chinese to carry out business with them in that language.

In sum, then, many of the narratives around learning Chinese are exaggerated or hugely over-simplified, while the serious difficulties of learning the language to a good standard (despite its morphological simplicity, the script and the tones present a real challenge) are underplayed. We do not at all think that learning Chinese is a bad idea – on the contrary, we think it's an excellent idea. But its benefits to the learner are *much* more likely to be the ones we talked about in Chapter 6, such as cultural enrichment, intercultural awareness, personal development, knowledge about language and so on than the ones that are routinely claimed for it.

7.2.3 So on what basis do we choose a language?

As should be clear from our discussion here and in the previous chapter, you could learn *any* language, to be honest, and most of the benefits would be approximately the same. In the end it comes down to the preference of the pupil, the culture of the school, its pupils and its surrounding area, and the availability of trained staff. The different languages all offer something different in cultural terms, and perhaps in employment terms (though this is almost impossible to quantify) – but all will provide a beneficial language learning experience, if they are taught with a wide intercultural focus and an emphasis on language awareness. This implies that motivation is probably the key factor: whatever language interests or excites a child most is the one that they should choose, and the one that interests the most children is probably the one that a school should aim to offer. Spanish, German, French, Chinese – it doesn't really matter, as long as the aims are realistic and the benefits are not oversold. In fact, it's so clear that communication is not often the primary goal, that you might find you are very well served by learning a language which has no native speakers at all – Latin. It's not an MFL, then, obviously enough, but we'll still throw it in for good measure.

One question that you might be asking, particularly if you teach in a multicultural environment, is: why do schools so often tend to stick to the traditional language offer, even where other languages are spoken in the community around them? What about Arabic, say, which was also mentioned by the British Council as one of the 'languages for the future'? What about Portuguese, for that matter, or Turkish or Polish or Urdu? This leads us on to the fuzzy line which divides 'foreign' and 'community' languages.

7.3 It's modern, it's foreign, and it's a language: language hierarchy and so-called 'community' languages

Urdu is modern, it's foreign, and it's certainly a language: so why isn't Urdu routinely considered to be a modern foreign language? Why isn't Cantonese, or Pashto, or Polish, or Turkish, or any of the other languages which are widely spoken in homes in British towns and cities? There has long been a perceived divide between these so-called 'community' languages and the 'traditional' languages (plus Arabic and Mandarin) that we looked at in the last section; and while the divide is not as marked as it used to be even a decade ago, it is still firmly there.

Officially, many groups and institutions do not recognise such a distinction at all these days, regarding it as implying a hierarchy of languages – and you would have to say, they've got a point. The DfE's website doesn't use the term, for example – it says specifically that the 'teaching of any modern or ancient foreign language' at school is acceptable. But ask most people what an MFL at school is and they are likely to volunteer one of French, German or Spanish (and perhaps Chinese). And everyone knows that a 'community language' is something else again.

The awkwardness of the divide shows itself in the awkwardness of the definitions that are in circulation. Tellingly, CILT (the National Centre for Languages, now closed down) used to define them as what they are *not*, that is not 'the more common, often western European languages taught in our education system and taken advantage of [sic] by employers'.[6] You can see why such a definition, spectacularly unhelpful as it was, came about, when you look at the alternatives. The webpage of NATECLA, the National Association for Teaching English and Other Community Languages to Adults, offers this:

> Where learners with basic literacy and study skills needs live in a community in which the target language is widely used, the language is termed a community language. Where learners learn a language for a social or work situations [sic], the target language is termed a Modern Foreign Language.[7]

The 'is termed' is problematic, of course: 'is termed' by whom, exactly, and on what grounds? But far more problematic is the suggestion that community languages are for people with 'basic literacy and study skills needs'. Does that mean that there will be little reading and writing in class, just conversation? What if the students want to learn to read and write the language, or want to learn it for 'social or work situations' within the community? Is it then a MFL? And where does all this leave the Turkish and Chinese Saturday schools, for example, which with backing from their national governments set out to instil full literacy in the official languages (of which more in a moment)?

Meanwhile a policy briefing on community languages and social cohesion by the MEITS ('Multilingualism: Empowering Individuals, Transforming Societies') project opens with:

> The term 'Community Languages' is used here to refer to the languages of the various immigrant communities in the UK, both longstanding and more recent. The term 'Heritage Languages' is sometimes also used for this purpose.[8]

This is frankly absurd, as a moment's thought will confirm. For example, Brazilian and most Angolan immigrants to London speak Portuguese, while many north and west African immigrants speak French. Are these, then, community languages? Are they still community languages if they are being spoken by Portuguese or French people, as opposed to people of the former colonial empires? Or are they then MFLs? Or does it depend on the context in which the language is taught, or on the aim of the teaching? Is Punjabi a MFL if it is taught at school for GCSE, while Portuguese is a community language if it is taught in a Saturday school to children of Angolan background? And if it's as simple as that, why doesn't everyone just say so?

It is a wholly confused and illogical picture, which is why many suspect that what really lies beneath the distinction between different 'kinds' of language is a bundle of social and cultural judgements, rather than a primarily pedagogic or linguistic demarcation. There exists a hierarchy or pyramid of languages, with a few languages at the top having more value than others in the eyes of society at large, for historical, cultural and political reasons. The other languages, mainly non-western European and associated with migrant groups or those of migrant background, are offered in mainstream schools only rarely, and in most parts of the country, never. If you do decide to welcome into the school languages from the surrounding community, either as straightforward MFLs leading to qualifications, or in the form of a Saturday school or after-school club or something similar, it is worth bearing in mind that the sociolinguistic background can be a complicated, politicised and even emotive one. And as we are about to see, it can require some informed and sensitive decision making.

7.3.1 What kind of language are we actually teaching?

When society values languages differently, it is no surprise that this is picked up on by the speakers themselves: people can be acutely aware of the lack of prestige that underpins the use of the term 'community', 'heritage' or 'home' language as opposed to modern foreign language. But there's another thing, and it can have big ramifications in the classroom and beyond. It's not always at all obvious, even to the genuinely well-intentioned outsider, but there is often a second level of discrimination and marginalisation in play here.

The 'community' languages are sometimes offered in mainstream schools, but just as often in supplementary schools (also sometimes known as complementary schools or Saturday schools), thousands of which operate in cities across the UK. These institutions tend to see it as their core mission to instil into younger generations of speakers the dominant national and cultural identity of their parents' homelands. They often use curricula and textbooks imported directly from the mother country, which tend to place heavy emphasis on the formal, standard or prestige variety, with its 'correct' grammar. And this, naturally, will very often differ markedly from the variety of the language spoken in the child's home. So while the intentions behind such language teaching might be sound – to increase the child's cultural confidence, to help maintain intergenerational ties, for example between grandchildren and grandparents, to encourage development of a settled bilingual and bicultural identity – there can be a yawning gap between the intention and what is actually delivered.

This is not to say that the ability to speak (and especially to read and write) the standard, formal language is not valued. It may well be valued, by parents and pupils alike, and the more so if it leads to a GCSE or other qualification. But the typical curriculum of this kind tends to neglect entirely the everyday, informal and non-standard varieties of the language, and therefore connects only partially with the lived experience of the child in their own speech community. This can apply to pretty much any language, of course, including English, as we have shown; but it is most clearly seen in those language communities where there exists a considerable distance (linguistically and socially) between a high-prestige standard and the regional dialect or other variety spoken in the home. We're going to take a quick dive into the sociolinguistics of that, as it has serious implications for what is supposedly 'home' language teaching – but you can skip to Section 7.4 if you're not interested.

As London-based Cypriot linguist Dr Petros Karatsareas explains it,[9] British-born Cypriot Greek speakers describe their heritage language using negative labels that are familiar from Cyprus, like *xorkática* ('villagey') and *varetá* ('heavy'). However – and this is the kind of detail that sociolinguists like! – they also use labels that have been borrowed from the way non-standard varieties of English are often described, such as *spazména* ('broken') or 'slang'. Much the same processes and ways of thinking can be seen in other communities. Take, for example, the relation between Sylheti (spoken by many British Bangladeshis) and standard Bengali. Sylheti is strongly associated with the rural village and a lack of education and sophistication, especially when compared to Bengali, with its long literary tradition, its Nobel Prize-winning poet Rabindranath Tagore (there is a bust of him in London's Gordon Square and another in Stratford-upon-Avon) and its status as the official language of Bangladesh and parts of India. Most British Turkish speakers are speakers of the Cypriot variety of the language, rather than the emphatically standard Turkish taught in north London supplementary schools and funded by the Turkish government. Children from Arab backgrounds will speak a Moroccan, Algerian, Syrian or whatever variety of Arabic at home rather than the literary or Modern Standard Arabic known as *fusha*. And so on, and on.

There's an unavoidable tension here, and a situation can quickly develop where the language used at home is felt to be undervalued or even denigrated by the school. Equally, the language which is taught at school might not be perceived by the children concerned to be part of their cultural identity. It can also be the case – though this is arguably a less common scenario – that parents (and perhaps) children want the prestigious national, 'proper' language to be taught, and are unimpressed with the idea of spending time learning something associated chiefly with illiterate people in remote villages. Teachers without adequate understanding and language awareness (many of them are enthusiastic volunteers with a limited pedagogic or sociolinguistic background) may be very well aware of the underlying disconnect, but lack the detailed knowledge, the will or the resources to tackle it in the classroom. The result is predictable. Children become disengaged and lose interest in the classes; they drop out, eventually they grow up as monolingual English speakers, and the link with the heritage language and culture is lost.

When approaching the question of 'community' languages in the sociolinguistically aware school, then, or when working with supplementary schools and other community language advocates, it is most important to bear these sensitive issues in mind. Specifically, it is important to speak directly and clearly to the teachers, as well as to pupils and their parents, about what *exactly* is to be taught. It is not enough to be told that 'we'll be teaching the children Turkish', say, or 'we want our children to learn Greek'. Volunteer teachers, to put it bluntly, might well have a political and/or linguistic agenda (and as one group of researchers put it, they can 'become vehicles for language ideologies in enacting monovarietal policies'[10]), and the parents may well also have preconceived ideas; so ground rules need to be agreed upon at the start. A language awareness approach to the issue would demand that the curriculum be flexible and realistic, and that the children be encouraged to develop an understanding of the social context of the language, not just taught what is officially 'correct'. This necessarily means that there should be discussion of standard and non-standard varieties, comparison of the taught form with the form spoken at home, and so on. In short, the complementary or community language classroom needs to be a sociolinguistically aware classroom: one that is welcoming of *all* aspects of the 'home' language as well as of the development of children's multilingual repertoires.

7.4 Primary languages: is earlier really better?

Virtually all primary schools in England are now teaching a MFL, since this was made compulsory at Key Stage 2 in 2014.[11] Some schools take it very seriously and do it very well (see 7.4.2 below). Others, though, struggle mightily, for a variety of reasons. The MEITS project that we mentioned earlier has detailed the problems existing in the sector, the key elements of which we can summarise as follows:

- The average amount of time spent on languages in primary schools is between 30 and 60 minutes per week – which, as we discuss further at 7.4.3 below, is not nearly enough to make any meaningful progress. However, in a good number of schools, even that low figure is not regularly reached, as competing priorities tend to squeeze out the language lessons.

- School leadership teams, governors and teachers might be unaware of, or just unconvinced by, the importance of languages across the curriculum. Languages are hence not seen as a core subject, and are neglected.

- Many teachers lack the skills, confidence and training to deliver the languages component of the curriculum. There is rarely a MFL pedagogy training component in primary PGCE courses, and CPD courses are insufficient.[12]

It is not a particularly happy picture. So are the resources put into this always sensibly used? Is it really the case that early language learning should have a central place in the primary school's strategic objectives? And underlying all this, the bigger question: how much do we really know about young children and language learning?

The belief that children learn another language quickly and effortlessly is so widespread as to seem like just common sense – it's almost universal. Or at least universal *among laypeople*. Most linguists who have actually studied the relationship between age and second language learning are much, much more sceptical about the whole thing. And this isn't just the usual academic caution – it's a lot more substantial than that. In fact, surrounding the notion of 'the earlier the better' there are a number of fundamental misconceptions, not to mention a good few half-truths and exaggerations. So much so, in fact, that once you dig into the question a little, you might find yourself thinking twice about the wisdom of investing too many of your school's resources in the vision of producing small children with fluent Mandarin or native-like French. Let's try to disentangle myth from reality, and establish what we really know about children and language learning.

At the root of the problem, you might not be surprised to hear, is the way a body of academic theory and research somehow became garbled in its journey from the university into popular consciousness.

7.4.1 Children and language learning

In the 1950s and 60s, amid an upsurge of academic interest in how children acquire language, neurologists and psychologists (in particular, Wilder Penfield and Lamar Roberts in their 1959 book *Speech and Brain Mechanisms*, whose themes were later widely popularised by Eric Lenneberg's 1967 *Biological Foundation of Language*) developed the so-called Critical Period Hypothesis. In essence, this theory suggested that there exists a 'window of opportunity' in the first few years of life, during which children acquire the language or languages spoken in the environment around them, without any active effort on their part. Once the window closes, and the critical period comes to an end – perhaps around the age of puberty, though there has been much debate about this – the ability to acquire language declines over time. And in fact, if children do not have adequate language input during these years, they will never learn to speak a language – any language – with full competence.

Research since has provided a fair amount of data to support the theory of the critical period, and many linguists would accept that, as a very general rule, your ability to absorb new language reduces with age. But here's the problem. As we've just noted, the theory dealt with the acquisition of your *first* language (or languages, if you grow up in a bilingual environment): that is, the language that surrounds you and in which you are immersed during your earliest years of life. But in the popular mind the theory was over-generalised and extended to the ability to learn further languages beyond that.

And so, gradually, it has begun to be established as a common sense fact – something that everyone simply *knows* – that children just 'pick up languages' easily, quickly and without effort, regardless of context, environment, motivation, amount of exposure, or any of the other complicating factors. That leads to half-truths and downright nonsense being peddled by parenting websites and commercial language teaching operations, playing on adults' awkwardness and embarrassment about their own lack of language skills and misrepresenting the academic consensus. Here's a prime example, from the Parent.Co. website:

> Do you hope for your child to have access to ideas and perspectives from another language? Do you dream of your son effortlessly switching between different languages as you sip Prosecco overlooking an Italian sunset?

You would have to admit, the Prosecco-sipping is a particularly nice touch. It goes on:

> Do you daydream about visiting Paris with a daughter who can negotiate like a local? Great! [...] Well, all researchers agree that the earlier a child starts learning a second language, the better, for more reasons than one... [T]hey all agree that it's much harder for a child beyond puberty to learn a new language.[13]

It is worth noting, of course, that the confusion developed in part because this idea seemed to fit with people's impressions of children and language: many people's observations and life experience suggest to them that children really do find second language learning easy. And it is true that children's neural connections are more flexible and plastic, allowing them to pick up native-like pronunciation, for example, with more ease than adults (though adults have other powerful advantages with language, such as the mature ability to compare grammatical structures). Young children moving to a new country with their families seem to make much faster progress than their parents, which is why you often hear things like: 'The little Polish boy who moved in next door has learned English so fast!' or 'My niece went to live in Spain and now she speaks Spanish just like a native!' But if you base your expectations of children's language learning at school on the performance of migrant children learning a language in an environment where it occurs naturally, then you're going to be sadly disappointed – because you're not comparing like with like.

Children who learn a second language in a fully immersive environment make fast progress in general because they have *massive* exposure to the target language – hour after hour, day after day, month after month. And this doesn't just go on at school, but continues in the society that surrounds them (the added exposure that linguists refer to as 'reinforcement'). They also, of course, have extraordinary motivation to learn, because they want to fit in and socialise with their peer group. The same learning mechanisms simply do not operate when the child is having a couple of lessons a week, in a classroom environment, with exposure to a single teacher, in a country where the language is not widely used. Now, quite a lot can be done in semi-immersive environments – which, of course, is why parents spend good money to send their children to the private bilingual schools that we mentioned at the beginning of Chapter 6. But let's get down to brass tacks. Linguist Dr Jenifer Larson-Hall classes anything below four hours' exposure a week as 'minimal input', and considers it likely to bear very little fruit, especially in the short term.[14] And then consider that 50 percent of primary schools actually teach languages each week for *less than 45 minutes*.[15] This is not to say that it is necessarily time wasted, as we will see in a moment, but it does mean that in terms of actual language learned, relatively little is going to be achieved.

To reiterate: if children seem to be able to pick up language quickly and easily, it is above all because they get vast amounts of exposure. From birth to the age of four, they might have some 17,000 hours of exposure to the home language.[16] If you were to reproduce that in the standard British MFL classroom, with 90 or so hours of learning annually, it would take 189 years! It's worth bearing that in mind next time you hear someone state confidently that early language learning is guaranteed to produce results because 'everyone knows' that children 'just pick up' language, or that 'young children's brains are like a sponge, they will soak up all the grammar rules and vocabulary that they are exposed to', as one tuition company's website claims.[17] Dr Karen Lichtman, a specialist in children and second language acquisition at Northern Illinois University, sums it up like this: 'People think that children are fast at learning language. They're not fast; they're slow.'

7.4.2 So is it a waste of time to teach primary MFL?

Well, is it a waste of time? Emphatically, no. There are positives, even if the conditions are not met for genuinely effective, substantial language learning. The key is to have reasonable expectations: in terms of actual language learned and retained over the long term, relatively little is going to be achieved. But you can focus on fostering motivation and enjoyment in language learning, raising language awareness, developing positive attitudes towards the target language and the community of people who speak the target language, and on acquiring cognitive and cultural benefits, as we saw in Chapter 6. Just don't expect instant results! It is going to take some time for the benefits to become apparent. And if primary language learning is to achieve real results of any kind, there need to be a set of circumstances in place. Here's the bare minimum: proper training and continuing professional development (CPD) for teachers, teachers with good language skills and a measure of language awareness, age-appropriate and stimulating materials and activities, guaranteed regular and frequent input, some reinforcement outside the classroom, and, not least, planning and liaison for the transition to secondary school, so that children do not end up being taught language that they have already learned or language that is too difficult.

These principles deserve to be absorbed by the management teams who decide when and how to introduce MFLs, and even by devolved governments of the UK. The government of Scotland, for example, has adopted the EU-mandated 1 + 2 model – meaning that all pupils should study their home language at primary school, plus two others – essentially on no more sound a basis than that the teachers and parents who were asked about this by questionnaire thought that early language learning was a good idea. One critical review of the policy quoted the reasoning involved: 'Two key rationales for the introduction of the policy... were the belief in the importance of having a second language in today's increasingly globalised world, and in the benefits of learning from a younger age.'[18] And indeed, 'belief' is perhaps the appropriate word here, as this is akin to an act of faith. The problems that the 1 + 2 project ended up running into, as described in that review – e.g. sustainability worries as funding was withdrawn, lack of continuity through to secondary school, teachers feeling untrained and unsupported – are illustrative of the dangers of policy making being guided by what appears to be misguided 'common sense' (and perhaps a desire to do some vigorous pro-EU political signalling), rather than by linguistically informed analysis.

What really helps a short-term experience of early language learning develop into a lifelong benefit, though, is a properly language-aware approach. Take the whole-school language policy adopted by Yeading Junior School in Hayes, Middlesex, as described in a report by the British Council[19]:

> The focus at Yeading is on language awareness and the acquisition of generic language skills, which is not only beneficial when learning the new language (in this case, French) but also English, home languages, and future languages the children will learn.

Note how language is integrated into the school curriculum as it is into the children's home lives, how the approach maximises exposure to language and languages, how it focuses firmly on 'generic language skills' and not just 'communication'. Crucially (remember our discussion in Chapter 6), note how it always has one eye on the child's *future* language needs. And that's not all:

> Language awareness permeates the school: in addition to the one hour per week in which all children learn French, every opportunity is taken to intro-

duce children to other languages, including Latin and the languages spoken by teachers and pupils.

The school explicitly values all languages equally, including those spoken at home by teachers and pupils. They even manage to throw in Latin – well, it was a modern foreign language once, too. This is evidently a school where the importance of language *as language* is thoroughly understood, and language issues are approached in an organised, integrated, even organic manner. The report notes: 'It is an ethos that firmly promotes bilingualism as an asset: as one pupil put it, "the more languages you know, the brainier you are"'. EAL pupils are therefore confidently welcomed, as they should be, of course:

> This school also caters for a similarly high proportion of pupils with English as an additional language, and sees language-learning as an integral part of their educational mission: 'It's part of who we are. It's part of our children's success'.

Such children are often withdrawn from MFL classes even though research, not to mention our own personal experience, suggests that such children serve as positive role models in the language classroom. Indeed, being experienced language learners, they often outperform other children in learning additional languages, and get a self-esteem boost in the process. As a member of staff at a Newcastle primary school put it in that same British Council report: 'children who may not speak much English can be as good as everyone else in Spanish'.

I (Tim) recall the awed expressions on the faces of English pupils in a beginners' German class at an east London comprehensive when some of their classmates, south Asian boys who had been in England only a matter of weeks, took to German like ducks to water. They may have been relatively new to English, but they were not new to language, or, especially, to the conceptual stretch involved in encountering and dealing with a new language. There are many reasons why a language-aware classroom welcomes all the linguistic resources that the pupils bring with them.

7.5 Conclusion

So which language and when? As we noted in 7.2.3 above, which language is probably not that important, really. If you, or pupils, or their parents are finding it very difficult to settle on a language or languages, it may well be that you're focusing on the wrong thing. Whatever feels most attractive, even if that's a very vague feeling, is going to be fine. The 'when' – or, more specifically, 'how much, when' – is a comparatively much trickier and more contentious issue, and it may be that some persuasion and some free-ranging discussion and even education is necessary in order to get everyone on board with what is finally decided.

A measured blog post by Professor Jean-Marc Dewaele of Birkbeck, University of London, entitled 'Why younger is not always better in foreign language learning' ends with a message for all those advocating early language learning, whether governments or school management teams: *Take the nuanced research findings into account, and avoid promising miracles.*[20] That's got to be sound advice. And we would add one more general piece of advice regarding MFL provision. Whenever your Parent Teacher Association, or a Governor, or whoever it might be, starts saying 'Everybody knows that…' – it might be a good idea to stop for a moment and think to yourself: actually, *do* we really know that?

Notes

1 https://www.simplylearningtuition.co.uk/advice-for-parents/when-to-start-learning-a-foreign-language/
2 Lo Bianco, J. & Slaughter, Y. (2009), *Second Languages and Australian Schooling.* Camberwell: Australian Council for Educational Research.
3 https://blog.keatschinese.com/7-reasons-why-learning-chinese-is-important/
4 https://www.china-admissions.com/blog/is-learning-chinese-worth-it/
5 https://www.kensingtonwade.com
6 See the discussion in English, F. & Marr, T. (2015), *Why Do Linguistics?* London & New York: Bloomsbury, p. 220.
7 https://www.natecla.org.uk/content/478/Community-languages
8 https://www.meits.org/files/policy_documents/uploads/POLICYBRIEFING COMMUNITYLANGUAGES.docx.pdf
9 https://www.thebritishacademy.ac.uk/publishing/review/33/fragile-future-cypriot-greek-language-uk/
10 Cushing, I., Georgiou, A. & Karatsareas, P. (2021), 'Where two worlds meet: language policing in mainstream and complementary schools in England'. *International Journal of Bilingual Education and Bilingualism.* DOI: 10.1080/13670050.2021.1933894
11 https://www.britishcouncil.org/sites/default/files/language_trends_survey_2015.pdf
12 https://www.meits.org/files/policy_documents/uploads/Policy_Briefing_on_Modern_Languages_Educational_Policy_in_the_UK.pdf
13 https://www.parent.com/blogs/conversations/the-best-age-for-kids-to-learn-a-second-language
14 Larson-Hall, J. (2008), 'Weighing the benefits of studying a foreign language at a younger starting age in a minimal input situation'. *Second Language Research* 241 (24): 35–63.
15 https://www.britishcouncil.org/voices-magazine/language-learning-decline-england-schools
16 Collins, L. & Muñoz, C. (2016), 'The foreign language classroom: current perspectives and future considerations'. *The Modern Language Journal* 100: 133–147.
17 https://www.simplylearningtuition.co.uk/advice-for-parents/when-to-start-learning-a-foreign-language/
18 Murray, E. (2017), 'Modern languages in Scottish primary schools: an investigation into the perceived benefits and challenges of the 1 + 2 policy'. *Scottish Languages Review* 33: 39–50.
19 https://www.britishcouncil.org/voices-magazine/compulsory-languages-primary-schools-does-it-work
20 http://blogs.bbk.ac.uk/research/2014/10/08/why-younger-is-not-always-better-in-foreign-language-learning/

8 In conclusion: What we can do to promote language awareness at school

8.1 Introduction: towards an integrated language policy

In subject-teaching terms, language awareness goes all the way from thinking about etymology and morphology (How come we sometimes use Latinate and sometimes Anglo-Saxon words for the same thing? And why do we say *fluvial* or *hydrology*?) up to discipline-specific grammatical features and textual organisation (the passive voice is a characteristic feature of lab reports; in discursive writing, paragraphs often begin with a topic sentence). Beyond that, though, as we have argued throughout this book, language awareness can inform multiple areas of school life, from attitudes to the use of Standard English to how best to approach issues like community languages and 'early start' foreign language teaching. Language awareness can help teachers build social justice – in terms, for example, of validating and helping students and other members of the school community to learn to value non-standard or stigmatised forms of expression, such as regional or ethnic dialect usage (remember our various mentions of Multicultural London English), or just unfashionably working-class accents. Language awareness might even help us with the problem of boys' relative lack of interest in English and writing compared to that of girls. Anecdotally, we know some of them warm to the 'Hallidayan' approach to thinking about language that we mentioned in Chapter 4 (see e.g. Section 4.4 and the 'Genre and regenring' text box in the same chapter) – an approach which focuses on what language does and what can be achieved with it, conceptualising words not primarily as decorative or expressive things, but as tools which can be used to make things happen, just as mixing two elements together can make things happen in the laboratory.

If we are to encourage language awareness at all levels and in all areas of school life, then those familiar mantras, 'all teachers are literacy teachers' and 'all teachers are English teachers', need to be rethought and repurposed. It is quite true that all teachers help teach literacy (and therefore English), but the issue of language in schools goes a good deal further than that. Language is not just English, and literacy – especially academic literacy – is not just about being able to read and write competently.

DOI: 10.4324/9781003201281-10

Nor is it just about mastering Standard English. In any case, most schools are already heavily invested in the notion of literacy as it is commonly understood, with literacy coordinators and the primary literacy hour (introduced back in 1998) and the like. In this book we have argued for a wider conception of what 'language issues' actually are, and a properly informed approach to dealing with them.

Schools need a framework of language knowledge and awareness in order to successfully meet students' language and communication needs, both now (not least because they have to pass high-stakes exams) and in the future (in order to function as adults in, and contribute to, complex societies). Who should have the responsibility for developing and leading this policy? As you will doubtless have noticed by now, we do not think language policy should lie in the hands of people who have no genuine knowledge of language. For example, to put it bluntly, and reiterating what we said right at the start of this book, it benefits nobody when academy heads, taking their lead from similarly uninformed government ministers, issue language diktats based on their own prejudices and misunderstandings. However, as will also by now have become clear, we do not think either that the responsibility for driving language awareness at school should lie solely with English departments.

This leads us to two recommendations, or conclusions, which you will find foregrounded in Sections 8.3 and 8.4 of this chapter. The first one is that all schools should aim to have a language coordinator, whose key duty would be to develop and drive an organised language policy. This might be someone in the English department, or it could be a Modern Foreign Languages teacher, or the existing Literacy Coordinator – but this person would take language awareness as seriously as they do literacy, because you cannot have one without the other. And it would have to be someone who – again, putting it bluntly – knows what they are talking about. There are certainly more than a few of these people around, in schools up and down the country. But in the medium to long term, more teachers will be in a position to take on this kind of role if a change happens at national level, which forms the basis of our second recommendation. This is that all teachers should have at least some language awareness training, both as part of their initial teacher training course and as continuing professional development throughout their career.

So we are talking about a shift in thinking: not a seismic one, but a considered adjustment to how we approach language issues in schools. And this, naturally, implies building in language awareness to teacher training and government education policy. Hence, in this concluding chapter, we concentrate on how to approach the development of language awareness in schools in pedagogic, organisational and policy terms, to arrive at a model of what the framework might look like at different levels. In Section 8.2 we reprise the principles that we discussed in Chapter 4, and look at the level of the particular subject and the individual classroom. In 8.3 we turn our attention to whole-school language policy, in particular the key roles of the Literacy Coordinator, the English department and the MFL department; and in 8.4 we discuss the place of linguistics and language awareness in teacher training and professional development. As part of this last, we will try to lay out a kind of compendium of language knowledge – a summary of what teachers and schools need to know about language.

8.2 Language awareness at the classroom and subject level

When planning lessons, it is formally the responsibility of each teacher to consider the Teachers' Standards, which they will have been instructed to use when they first embark on their ITT course, whether they have taken the traditional PGCE or BEd route or come via schemes such as School Direct or Teach First. These range from, for example, 'Plan and teach well-structured lessons' and 'Manage behaviour' to 'Make accurate use of assessment'. The key standard here for our purposes is: 'Demonstrate an understanding of and take responsibility for promoting high standards of literacy, articulacy and the correct use of standard English, whatever the teacher's specialist subject.' We need to build into any lesson in any subject a number of factors, which can be encapsulated in the 5-minute lesson plan template recommended by the DfE.[1] According to this skeletal but effective and adaptable plan, all lessons should include things like a 'big picture', objectives, stickability, adaptive learning (how are the needs of children of all abilities met?), assessment for learning (how are understanding and progress checked?) and so on. Teachers also need to take any opportunity available to encourage numeracy, and consider any key words the students need to learn and use.

However, as we have pointed out elsewhere (see in particular Chapter 4), academic literacy goes well beyond the concept of 'key words' or specialist terminology, important though this certainly is. We would argue that other language features should also be clearly and explicitly taught. What we are talking about, then, might be called 'key language' and would encompass questions like: what different grammatical features are present at various stages of the lesson? How do these features work and what do they help us to do? In this regard, schools would find it helpful to look at the methodologies routinely employed in the fields of Content and Language Integrated Learning (CLIL) and Teaching with English as the Medium of Instruction (TEMI). These approaches are well established in English-using schools and universities in countries where English is not the first language, and place the principle of language learning and consolidation at the centre of their teaching. A key element – in fact, *the* key element – is that for every lesson, language learning objectives are explicitly set alongside content objectives in the teacher's lesson plan.

Let's see what language-aware lesson planning might look like.

8.2.1 Language-aware lesson planning

How do we go about embedding language awareness into, say, a science lesson based around an experiment? As a starter, pupils could look at some of the morphology and etymology of typical words used in the field. The teacher and blogger Dr Joanna Rhodes demonstrates language use in science at the teachsecondary.com website with the example of the word *nephros* (Greek for kidney), explaining how the root word is used to describe different 'situations' that a kidney can be found in (*nephralgia* for pain in the kidney, *nephritis* for inflammation of the kidney and so on). For the next, main part of the lesson, students learn to use some of the language of experimentation: *variables, hypothesis, control, error* and *anomalous*, which all lead into the concept of 'working scientifically', shared by all three sciences at GCSE. After conducting an experiment to test a hypothesis, students are reminded to use certain grammatical structures in the writing up of the experiment: sequential discourse markers; imperatives; modal auxiliaries; the passive voice; 'if' clauses, for instance. The lesson includes a homework task in which students read a science article (*The Day*[2] is a reliably good source), underline any of the relevant features used in the article, and perhaps use these structures in a piece of their own writing.

All this language work can be effectively generated by the use of a planning template which focuses the teacher on the relevant language features at each stage of the lesson. A lesson plan template, then, might look something like this (Figure 8.1):

It's not a huge change from the standard kind of lesson plan template, but it adds a valuable language focus. As a follow-up elsewhere in the curriculum, in English lessons students could be set homework in which they read a text about a scientific discovery in the news and analyse how it uses particular grammatical

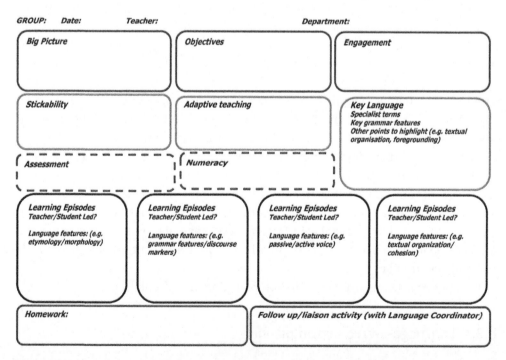

Figure 8.1 A language-aware lesson plan template, adapted from 5minutelessonplan.co.uk

structures; as you can see, liaison with other departments is explicitly included in the lesson plan too (we'll explain 'Language Coordinator' in just a moment). This kind of thing could be done for any subject, with the English department liaising with other departments to ensure that whatever is being taught in those lessons is followed up in a language awareness-based English homework. Alternatively, the English team could set a homework task of this kind each fortnight or half-term, thereby creating explicit language links between subjects – it doesn't have to take over the whole English curriculum.

All of this links very easily to what has been a recent welcome change in schools, as faculties have been required to create so-called 'Learning Journeys'. Each department produces these maps of progress, which help students, their parents, and also colleagues to understand what children are learning at any point in their school life. This encourages the kind of language planning and dovetailing that we have illustrated here, easing the process of making those crucial links, and thus aiding the whole idea of consolidated learning that we discussed above (and remember our Text Box in Chapter 4). Learning Journeys could make explicit reference to the types of language required during each phase of the journey: when will students need to write a formal essay, give a presentation or write up a science experiment, and what will be required of them linguistically when they do? When it comes to 'stickability', this is surely an ideal way for children to remember what they have learnt.

8.3 From literacy to language: mechanisms and structures for implementing language awareness at whole-school level

The current debate about the 'word gap' (as discussed in Chapter 4) has helped many of us to focus on the need for a more coherent and informed vision of how to make our students better communicators. For us, this means establishing a philosophy of language awareness across the school, including everyone from the senior leadership team to teaching assistants. In this section, as outlined at 8.1 above, we will start with one of our main recommendations for implementing this vision: the creation of a post in every school which carries the responsibility for promoting language awareness across the subjects and in the institution as a whole. We'll then look at some of the other obvious structural elements involved in embedding language awareness at school, and specifically the roles of the English and MFL departments. We will end the section in what we hope is a logical way, by floating a further suggestion for change. This is the restructuring of the 'language' areas of the school at departmental or faculty level so that they begin to work together on transforming the way the school approaches language issues. This is, admittedly, a potentially much more difficult and demanding change than simply appointing a 'language person' – though it's one which could bring great benefits – and we therefore suggest it as something which might be a fruitful area for future discussion, rather than as something which should be implemented immediately.

8.3.1 The role of the Coordinator

The most straightforward way for a school to begin the process of becoming a language-aware school is to have a member of staff, preferably one who has been awarded a Teaching and Learning Responsibility (TLR) allowance, to lead on language awareness throughout the school. Most schools already have, in one guise or another, a Literacy Coordinator, whose role it is to support literacy across the curriculum. For example, when new teachers and PGCEs start at a school, the Literacy Coordinator often provides some CPD input about the requirement to use Standard English in their teaching. But we would argue that the role of the Literacy Coordinator should not be restricted to developing a student's capabilities in reading and writing. It needs also to include the development of a student's capacity to write in a manner that is appropriate to the discourse of each particular subject, as well as being able to deal with the more general academic register expected across all subjects. And there is plainly a need for a competent person in each school to act in an advisory capacity on whole-school matters such as the use of Standard English and 'speaking in complete sentences', as well as liaising with the MFL department and community representatives to help develop integrated approaches to language and languages. In short, we suggest that the role of the Literacy Coordinator be widened and developed to include the responsibility for promoting language awareness across the school. They could, perhaps, be given the title of Language Coordinator – or LangCo, for short!

Who will deliver the language awareness programme in schools? Who would take on the role of the LangCo? Those most qualified, and ideally someone with some background in linguistics or at least the interest to develop their knowledge of the area. We would expect that either the English or the MFL departments (or, as we shall suggest in a moment, a combination of these) would be driving the language awareness initiative and so the Language Coordinator would most likely come from one of these faculties. However, the role might even suit an NQT who has enjoyed and been inspired by some of the language awareness resources that we have mentioned at different points in this book – and eventually, with any luck, the kind of language awareness course we will be proposing that all trainee teachers undertake, as laid out in 8.4 below.

The LangCo would naturally be the link between the English/MFL departments and the subject specialists, not only advising but also coordinating the production of subject-specific language awareness resources. As to what else, exactly they would do – well, there are plenty of options. They could lead half-termly meetings and workshops between faculty-based literacy/language leads and the senior leadership team to discuss language issues. They might drive weekly, monthly or termly initiatives, such as: promoting discussion about the use of Standard English, slang and vernacular English; helping develop language awareness resources in each department; raising awareness about different accents and home languages; organising Linguistic Olympiad puzzles in form time or in extra-curricular clubs.

For support and fresh ideas, the LangCo could set up links with LASER (Language Analysis in Schools: Education and Research)[3] and the International Linguistics Olympiad[4] – the former promoting language awareness in schools and the latter running linguistics competitions that school clubs can enter. The LangCo would also arrange and lead appropriate whole-school CPD training at INSETs.

8.3.2 The role of the English department

The English department has a two-fold role in the process of positioning the school as a language-aware institution. It has a central part to play in helping the LangCo and other department teachers in identifying and meeting their language needs; at the same time, its members have the bread-and-butter teaching job of raising language awareness in their own classrooms.

In the school

The shift from being in charge of literacy to being in charge of language is potentially a large one, but it is not actually a substantial change of direction. In fact, it is directly relevant to the obligation to ensure that 'high standards of literacy, articulacy and correct use of standard English' as required by the Teachers' Standards are maintained and promoted. As we have already noted, the LangCo needn't be an English teacher – but still, every member of the English teaching team should have a whole-school role in helping colleagues to improve understanding of language in the very broadest sense.

If English teachers are to take on this joint responsibility for language policy within the school, this necessarily means that they be language specialists, and position themselves as such (which, of course, does not prevent them being literature specialists too!). English teachers need to possess a properly informed understanding of how language works, both at the level of structure and at the level of language in society. At the very least, this would ensure that more English teachers felt empowered to raise their voices and push back against the palpable nonsense of, say, 'speaking in full sentences', or 'banning slang', as we discussed in the first half of the book. Where English teachers don't routinely have the linguistic knowledge and experience to be able to challenge these ill-founded and misguided 'literacy' initiatives, the entire teaching profession is left vulnerable to the heavily promoted arguments of people like Doug Lemov. They might well know that there's something wrong about such initiatives, but they don't always have the technical terms and theoretical foundations to be able to explain quite *why* they're wrong (and even harmful). And therefore they can't persuade others.

We have already suggested that the English department assist other faculties by setting regular homework tasks that focus on the linguistic requirements of a task set in another subject. But English could also help by liaising with other colleagues when they are thinking about language needs at the termly planning stage. Here, they could take another leaf out of the book of the EAP/TEMI methodologies we referred to above, and plan for meetings between departments to discuss language needs in each subject. Specifically, English specialists could meet subject teachers and ask them: what do your students need to do, linguistically speaking? Will they need to give spoken presentations, write essays or reports, describe processes, define concepts? What kind of language do they need to use? What do they need to *do* with the language? Then the English department can help them with strategies and even resources. In order to avoid an increased workload, this could be done at INSETs or during faculty meetings: maybe just a short 15-minute visit from the English department team in which they learn what the key language features in a subject are and discuss how they might be taught.

In the classroom

Meanwhile, of course, English teachers are still required to model language awareness in their own lessons, whether they are teaching an aspect of English language explicitly, or noticing linguistic patterns in a literary text. In this way, the good (if perhaps uneven) groundwork that has been done at KS2 can be built upon at KS3 and KS4. We have already discussed the excellent resources produced by the EMC in Chapter 5, but there is so much else that could be done to enhance language awareness even in literature-focused lessons, such as studying the demotic non-standard English in the poetry of John Agard and Tony Harrison, or in the fiction of Angie Thomas, who interweaves AAVE with Standard American English in *The Hate U Give*, or Alex Wheatle, who uses MLE in *Crongton Knights*. And – we are, of course, not the first people to recommend this – how about critical, informed class discussions about the attempts by some schools to ban certain words and phrases, discussed in Chapters 1 and 2? How about a project looking at local accents and dialects, or about the historical development of Standard English?

8.3.3 The role of the MFL department

MFL departments have an obvious role in enhancing grammatical literacy. As we noted in Chapter 5, the real point of learning grammar is to have a shared language, the metalanguage to talk about language. This has applications across all subjects (for everyone has to talk about language to some extent), but of course it has particular importance where the subject is actually a language. MFL teachers tend to be strong in grammar, and comfortable with talking about grammar, in a way that some English teachers are not. This could put them in a position to support and help drive detailed language work across the subjects – for example, in collaborating with subject departments in the way we mentioned at 8.3.2 above, or helping design the kind of academic style guides that we looked at in Chapter 4 ('how to write like a historian', or 'write like a scientist').

Of course, this might not suit every MFL teacher; but their remit could potentially be much broader than this, even going beyond the classroom. As we noted in Chapters 6 and 7, foreign language teaching brings to the fore interculturality, putting oneself in others' shoes, learning to see the world from other viewpoints besides your own. The skill set of a MFL teacher should mean that they are in a prime position to help in, for example, creating a welcoming environment for the students' home languages, acknowledging and valuing the linguistic repertoires of students, teachers and parents alike, making links with the languages spoken in the wider local community. All of this is part of building a language-aware school, from classroom level upwards.

An effective whole-school language policy, in other words, would harness the skills, insights and experience of MFL teams to those of the English department. Why does this sort of thing not already happen as a matter of course? Or, more specifically, why is there so rarely a shared 'language expert' identity among those who teach about language? Part of the answer lies in the fracture bequeathed by the language-versus-literature divide, which applies to at least some extent to MFL rather as it does to English. Part, too, in the frustratingly low profile of linguistics at school level and beyond, which has been repeatedly bemoaned by academic linguists and the teachers who share their concerns and goals (and which has given rise to things like the LASER network). Then there is the inevitable 'silo-ing' effect of schools being divided up administratively into separate departments – and, of course, the eternal bugbear of teachers' heavy workloads, which can dampen the desire for any kind of extra projects or initiatives. But where MFL teachers and English teachers alike recognise that an essential part of their professional identity is 'language specialist', then what corporate types like to call 'synergies' begin to emerge. Where might this end up? Well...

8.3.4 English and MFLs – an integrated faculty?

In all the schools I (Steve) have worked in, the English department has been administratively and even physically connected to either drama or maths. Both of these seem obvious links: the former due to the overlaps in content (we often study the same or similar drama texts, with drama focusing on the performative and English on the literary aspects of drama); the latter because both maths and English are 'core' subjects and a school's performance in these subjects provides a benchmark as to how successful a school is. Links like these are fairly common across schools: meanwhile, though, MFL often remains separated off in glorious isolation and, depending on the outlook of the school, is either left to its own devices or enthusiastically promoted.

But why exactly are English and languages virtually always separate departments? Biology, chemistry and physics, after all, always reside under the same departmental umbrella of 'science'. Is there not a case for a combined 'languages' department, where colleagues would put language awareness at the forefront of all teaching and, for example, focus on the delivery of the teaching of grammar in different contexts? At A Level, students might study texts in any of, say, English, German, Spanish, French and possibly Latin. Resources and strategies could be shared. Dialogue and shared understanding between colleagues would help set English literature firmly within a wider European and even non-European context. A context of intertextuality, whereby links between texts are explored and made explicit, could be extremely fruitful: you understand Poe better if you have read some Baudelaire, and vice versa!

8.4 Implementing language awareness at the national level

In this section, we first look at how language awareness might be integrated into teacher professional development and initial teacher training. Following this, we put forward some recommendations for policy change in areas, including the role and definition of Standard English and the content of GCSE English.

8.4.1 Integrating language awareness into teacher education and professional development: what do all teachers need to know about language?

Back in 2000, two academic researchers in educational linguistics were contracted by the US Department of Education to consider the question of how best to provide integrated training and professional development for American teachers in the area of language. Their published report was called *What Teachers Need to Know About Language*.[5] In it, having discussed the social and educational background (e.g. higher literacy benchmarks, increasing numbers of non-English-speaking children entering the school system, debates around bilingual education) they recommended that courses in several areas should be offered to teachers ('Courses That Teachers Need To Take'). The areas they selected were as follows:

1. Language and linguistics for educators

2. Language and cultural diversity

3. Sociolinguistics for educators in a linguistically diverse society

4. Language development

5. Second language learning and teaching

6. The language of academic discourse

7. Text analysis and language understanding in educational settings

It is worth stressing that the list was not put forward as core knowledge for English teachers, or language teachers, but as a basic set of requirements for *all* teachers, throughout the public education system, from kindergarten to high school. Now, this was admittedly an exercise in blue-skies thinking. The researchers acknowledged in their conclusion that their proposal 'may strike some readers as utopian' and admitted cheerfully that they made the proposal 'without thinking about the structures and constraints of traditional teacher education programs'. But that said – how much of it actually does represent desirable core knowledge for educators? You could probably lose 'second language learning and teaching' without too much grief (unless you teach MFL, obviously) and 'language development' is rarely a crucial concern beyond primary early years; but the rest is, to varying degrees, the sort of stuff that really should be part of a teacher's intellectual and practical toolkit. It's difficult to argue that teachers of any subject should not, for example, have at least a basic awareness of the sociolinguistics of multilingual and multicultural societies, or of what characterises the language of academic discourse.

In fact, the only real reservations we would have about this list are that it is quite general, and that it springs from a distinctively American context (which becomes clear if you read the whole report – there is discussion e.g. of 'Ebonics', and the particular needs of Latin American and southeast Asian children). But in that spirit of blue-skies utopianism, leaving aside just for a moment the question of financial and other constraints, let's try and put some flesh on the bones, and imagine what a similar toolkit of core knowledge for teachers in British schools might consist of.

Our putative course could have four main elements, making it look something like this:

Unit 1: Language and linguistics for teachers

The first unit of the course is an introduction to the study of language, organised around educational issues which involve language in some way. So while we have the word 'linguistics' in the title, we wouldn't envisage a 'Linguistics 101'-type course of the kind typically taught to undergraduates. There wouldn't be any need to teach the IPA, then, or to delve into the technical details of areas like semantics, pragmatics, or prosody. Rather, the aim is to raise awareness of language issues, and show how the discipline of linguistics can help to shed light on them – rather as we have tried to do in this book. You might look at how speaking and writing differ from a linguistics perspective, for example, and consider the implications of this for policies such as 'Students must answer in complete sentences'. You might discuss the case of a child reading aloud in their normal regional accent, as we did in Chapter 2, and talk about how insights from linguistics can help teachers focus on what 'reading aloud' is actually for.

Unit 2: Sociolinguistics and the school

This is essentially a condensed, schools-focused version of a primer course on language in society, aimed in large part at dispelling some of the myths and prejudices that so often dominate conversations about language. It would take as its core content the notions of standard language, non-standard language, accent, dialect and so on, and put them in the sort of social and historical context that sociolinguists take for granted. Hence we look at the notion of standard language ideologies, and trace the development of what we today call Standard English from its medieval origins. Ideas about 'speaking properly' or 'speaking clearly' and 'banning slang' would be worked through, and common prejudices against certain regional accents and (especially youth) sociolects examined from an informed sociolinguistic perspective. The unit would hence cover the central topic of language and identity in the context of 'micro-sociolinguistics', i.e. language variation according to social class, sex, gender identity, identification with certain speech communities, and so on. It would also include a brief overview of some 'macro-sociolinguistic' topics, notably World Englishes and the historical development of English as a global lingua franca.

Unit 3: Academic language and academic writing

This unit would focus on the register of academic discourse in general – and especially on how it differs from informal or non-specialist registers – and go on to look at the characteristic ways in which particular subjects produce and organise written texts. It would invite reflection on the various genres of academic communication ('What kind of text is this? Why is it written and organised in this way?') and reinforce the principle that children's higher-level language development is a shared responsibility of all teachers.

Unit 4: Bilingualism and language diversity

The purpose of this unit is to provide all teachers with a basic understanding of the needs, abilities and repertoires of bilingual/EAL children. It can, of course, come across as glib or facile to say that 'children's additional languages are a resource rather than a problem'. At the very least, though, a course of this kind should aim at emphasising that bilingual children, even those who have little English when they come to the school, are not simply 'deficient', linguistically speaking: they are actively engaged in the process of developing an expanded linguistic repertoire. The unit would cover typical bilingual behaviours such as code-switching or code-mixing and translanguaging, and encourage teachers to regard such behaviours as normal rather than problematic. It would guide teachers through some of the factors associated with the use of a particular home or 'heritage' language, such as domains of use and societal language attitudes. And it might also offer some simple, practical strategies for supporting bilingual/EAL children, such as not forcing them to speak, using support worksheets, allowing preparation time, facilitating group work, allowing use of the mother tongue, and so on.

Ideally, all teachers would have something like this kind of basic linguistics training (Language Awareness, Knowledge About Language, Educational Linguistics, or call it what you will) as part of their Initial Teacher Training (ITT), whether this be in the form of a PGCE, a BEd, a Teach First programme or something else. And indeed, a compulsory language awareness element in ITT is something that academics and others have called for repeatedly – over decades, in fact. Is it not time that such provision be made for teachers of any subject? Giovanelli and Clayton's *Knowing About Language: Linguistics and the Secondary English Classroom* focuses on the English classroom, as the title suggests, but its general drift is very much in the direction of language awareness as an integral part of all teacher education and practice. Meanwhile, cross-subject language awareness has long been a central concern of teacher trainers working in international education, with pupils whose first language is not English – see, for example, Cambridge International Education's useful website *Getting Started with Language Awareness*.[6] But it really needs to be a visible presence beyond the ITT stage, in INSETs and in CPD in general. And not just for classroom teachers: as we saw from the examples in Chapter 1 and then throughout the book, it is of the first importance that academy heads, senior leadership teams and other school decision-makers take this kind of course in order to inform their approaches to such matters as Standard English and the speech of their pupils. It wouldn't do any harm if some school governors were to take it, too – just a thought! And naturally, anyone who is at all involved in literacy development needs to have some basic awareness of how language works, including TAs (remember our story of the TA listening to a child read in Chapter 2). It's really a bit strange that this even needs to be said – but it does.

Once again, to be clear: we're not advocating a course in theoretical linguistics for everyone, with syntactic tree diagrams and the like. Language awareness means just that – an increased awareness of the language that surrounds us, an increased ability to notice linguistic phenomena and some basic tools and terminology to be able to analyse, interpret and talk about them. How might this course be delivered? Well, ideally it would run as an integral part of a PGCE, BEd or PGDE course, with the same kind of time and resources allocated to it as areas like, say, behaviour management or current educational issues. Realistically, though, such time may not be available: as many linguists have regretfully pointed out, it is very hard to interest policy makers in language as such, rather than 'Standard English' or 'literacy'. So you could teach this as a stand-alone module of, say, one or two weeks in duration. You could even cover the basics of it in a couple of days – anything is better than the current nothing, after all. **And what would we call it? Well – 'Language Awareness For Teachers' seems to pretty much sum it up**.

8.4.2 Further recommendations

We have nearly finished setting out our linguistic stall, but we do have one final bundle of recommendations to make.

At policy level

There is a genuine need for a clearer, more accurate, and more linguistically nuanced definition of Standard English in all government policy documentation (see Chapter 2). You can tell how strongly we feel about the importance of understanding what Standard English actually is: in Chapters 2 and 3 alone we use the term 100 times! Everyone, including heads and *all* teachers and teaching assistants, indeed anyone who interacts with children at school, should share this same understanding. We could start with a very short version:

> Standard English is the name given to a substantially regularised variety of English which over time has come to be regarded as broadly acceptable and understood wherever English is used. It is the form most often associated with educated or formal speaking or writing – though it can be spoken in any accent, and the spoken and written forms are not always identical.

And by the same token, everyone must be clear about what Standard English isn't. It isn't another way of saying 'correct' or 'proper' English. It's not clearer or more articulate than other ways of speaking. And it is not a benchmark by which regional, non-standard and working-class speech should be judged and found wanting. This should be specifically taught as part of a critical, language-aware approach to English, and needs to be understood by *all* concerned – including the Secretary of State for Education.

At exam level

As far as national exams are concerned, we would hope that with language awareness strategies embedded in the work of the school, there would in due course be a measurable improvement in written answers in GCSEs across the board. Clearly, though, it will be the English GCSEs that are primarily used to assess children's improved understanding of how language works. This means that these exams need to be repurposed in a way that shows real respect for and attention to the full range of language activity.

In order to move at least some way towards this we would like to see:

1. Adoption in full of the recommendations for reform of GCSE English Language made by NATE in 2021, which we discussed in Section 5.6.3 of Chapter 5.

2. Inclusion at KS3 and KS4 of a greater variety of writing tasks, for different purposes and audiences.

3. Reinstatement of the 'Study of Spoken Language' and 'Knowledge About Language' elements of the curriculum, including, for example, the study of accent and dialect (because when we say language, we don't just mean literacy!).

4. Reinstatement of 'Speaking and Listening' as an integral part of the English Language GCSE (removed from the GCSE requirements in 2014 and now assessed separately as the hopelessly misconceived 'Spoken Language Endorsement').

Bitzer's way with facts

In a recent Spoken Language Assessment with my Year 10s, I (Steve) was struck by how some of the students seemed to have no difficulty remembering facts but were far less sure about how to create a coherent discourse out of them. I was reminded of the character at the beginning of Dickens' *Hard Times*, Bitzer, the schoolboy who, when asked, can confidently describe a horse as: 'Quadruped. Graminivorous. Forty teeth, namely twenty-four grinders, four eye-teeth, and twelve incisive…' The same children who perform well in subjects which don't require them to speak at length, become tongue-tied when asked to speak to an audience of even five or six of their peers. What is it that is preventing them from being articulate? It's not words; it's register, awareness of the audience, the ability to construct a cohesive discourse, and, at the bottom of all this, confidence. A language-aware teacher will recognise this and help the student overcome this hurdle by building up their communicative abilities. And what's more, we believe that if a speaking and listening assessment to the GCSEs were reinstated, this whole crucial area of assessment might be given more weight and taken more seriously.

8.5 Conclusion

We are not going to attempt to reprise here all the reasons why language awareness is a good idea. If we haven't convinced you by now, we're unlikely to do so at this point. But let us leave you with a few final thoughts.

At the most basic level, language awareness might simply mean not having a prescriptive and discriminatory attitude towards others' speech – and this goes for all, including teachers, students and the government of the day. It is always worth bearing in mind that non-standard and informal does not necessarily mean incorrect, and that some aspects of language change rapidly. If there are elements of students' language usage that you strongly dislike, that doesn't necessarily mean that there is something wrong with the students' language: it might simply be that you have a prejudice against it. And, of course, you are perfectly entitled to have prejudices about language, just as you are about stripey trousers, say, or country and western music. However, it is a good idea, first, to acknowledge that these are indeed prejudices; and second, to keep them to yourself. I (Tim) don't happen to like the phrase 'My bad'. I (Steve) cringe when I hear children and adults asking me 'Please may you…' – however, now that I've even noticed this piece of 'hyper-politeness' used by a pension company in a letter I received, I've decided it's time to let go! Clearly, we can't like everything that people say, or how they say it, but neither should we criticise people who say things differently to us.

This is surely part of the discussion about language that should be happening at all schools. The classroom and the school function as natural sites for noticing

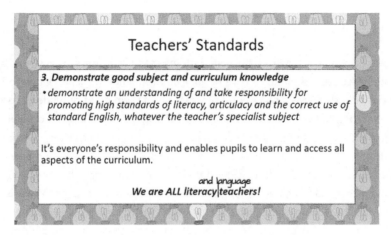

Figure 8.2 Amended slide from a Teachers' Standards presentation.

and talking about language, for exploring language behaviour in all its facets. There is therefore a strong case for schools to be open to, and properly informed about, language issues of all kinds – including the students' own use of language. Awareness of language should flourish at the centre of school life, thus helping to develop students' communicative skills and make them more effective, confident and informed users of language.

At my (Steve's) school, and presumably at most, all NQTs, trainees and PGCEs are required to attend an INSET course called Literacy Across The Curriculum. During this they are reminded about Teachers' Standard number 3, with a slide that ends: 'We are ALL literacy teachers!'. When I was tasked with delivering this session, after ensuring after thorough discussion that teachers knew and agreed what Standard English actually is, I made one small amendment to the slide, as you can see (Figure 8.2):

We are ALL literacy AND language teachers!

Notes

1 See http://www.5minutelessonplan.co.uk
2 https://theday.co.uk/
3 https://clie.org.uk/
4 https://ioling.org/
5 Fillmore, L. & Snow, C., (2000), *What Teachers Need To Know About Language*. Washington, DC: Center for Applied Linguistics.
6 https://www.cambridge-community.org.uk/professional-development/gswla/

Glossary

allophone In phonology, an allophone is a variant realisation of a phoneme in a particular language or dialect which does not change the meaning of a word. For example, in some British varieties of English the /t/ sound in *beaten* is realised as a glottal stop (['biʔən]) and in some American varieties as an alveolar tap (['birən]). For these varieties, then, [ʔ] and [ɾ] are among the allophones of the phoneme /t/.

appropriacy Appropriacy in linguistics refers to the extent to which a language feature such as a word, phrase or grammatical structure is considered to be fitting or suitable for the social context in which it is used.

clause A grammatical unit of language consisting of at least a subject and a verb (e.g. 'She's working').

code-switching Also *code-mixing* (sometimes the two are distinguished, sometimes not). The act or process of switching from one language, variety or register to another in the course of a conversation.

cognate A word that has the same historical derivation as a word in another language, such that they share the same linguistic ancestor: e.g. English *fish* and Danish *fisk*, or French *père* and Portuguese *pai*.

collocation Collocations are groups of two or more words that tend to occur together frequently, such as *pay attention* or *heavy rain*.

creole A creole is a fully-formed, natural, stable language that has arisen from a mixing of other languages. Creoles are very often the result of pidgin varieties having acquired native speakers over time and become the main or sole language of a population.

dialect A rule-governed, systematically-differing variety of a language shared by a particular group of speakers, usually geographical in nature.

diglossia This term is used to describe a situation where two languages or varieties are routinely used in different contexts within the same society, usually in the form of a 'high' and a 'low' variety.

digraph A digraph is a combination of two letters which together make a single sound, such as *ch* or *ph*.

discourse (first or narrower meaning) Language in use – examples of authentic stretches of language, spoken or written, collected and used for the purposes of analysis.

discourse (second or broader meaning) The characteristic features associated with a particular text type or area of communication.

domain In sociolinguistics, domain refers to a particular context (it might be physical, social or psychological) in which a particular language or variety is favoured or tends to be used. In situations of *diglossia* (see above), certain domains are associated with the 'high' language (typically such areas as government, higher education, literature) and others with the 'low' (for example, the home, initial education, jokes, folk tales).

English as a Lingua Franca (ELF) ELF refers to the use of English as an intercultural medium of communication, mainly among non-native speakers of the language. As a field of study, it emphasises the functional communicative practice of speakers rather than strict adherence to native-like forms of grammar and models of pronunciation.

filler A sound, word or phrase used when speaking to help us to think and/or organise our meaning (*um, er, like, so, basically, you know* etc.)

genre What kind of text is it: what does it look like, what is it for and what does it do? Genres are textual practices that have emerged from social and cultural activity, such as poems, sermons, academic essays or lab reports.

glottal stop In phonetics, the glottal stop (written in the International Phonetic Alphabet as /ʔ/) is produced when the glottis (the space between your vocal cords) is closed, stopping the airstream from the lungs for a fraction of a second. It often replaces a /t/ sound, as in /ˈbɒʔəl/ for *bottle*, or /ˈlɪʔəl/ for *little*. In Yorkshire, though, it can replace the word *the*, a feature often represented inaccurately in writing as *t'* – as in *trouble at t' mill*.

grammar Technically, the study of the interaction between *morphology* (the forms of words) and *syntax* (the rules governing how words are put together to create meaningful utterances and sentences in a given language).

International Phonetic Alphabet (IPA) An internationally recognised system of phonetic notation which gives speech sounds in all languages a standardised written symbol. It is based on the Latin script and was first devised in the nineteenth century.

mitigation Mitigation is the name given to the linguistic strategies we use to avoid face-threatening situations or to soften the impact of writing or speaking which might be unwelcome to the addressee. They include e.g. hedging, euphemism, indirectness and impersonal grammatical constructions.

modal verbs The auxiliary verbs in English that are used with other verbs to express such things as necessity, permission, possibility and obligation. Modal verbs include *can, could, must, should* and *might*.

mode Mode refers to the manner of communication (speech, writing, gesture, facial expression etc.)

morpheme   The smallest lexical items in a particular language which can carry meaning. *Free* morphemes can stand alone (*elephant, walk, hope*), while *bound* morphemes must be affixed to a word (for example, *-ly, un-, -s*).

morphology   The branch of linguistics which deals with the form and internal structure of words.

Multicultural London English *or* MLE   A sociolect of English which emerged in 1990s London, mainly in areas characterised by high immigration and ethnic diversity. It is based on working-class Cockney, but is heavily influenced by Caribbean (especially Jamaican) pronunciation and slang, as well as South Asian and West African usages.

multimodal, multimodality   A communicative event or text comprising more than one mode. (e.g. a text message involving writing and emoji; a video involving speech, music, gesture etc.).

parsing   This is when we describe the syntactic role played by the different words used in a clause or clause complex. (e.g. subject, verb, object).

parts of speech   This refers to the naming of different word functions (noun, pronoun, article, adjective, adverb, preposition, conjunction).

phoneme   The smallest distinct unit of sound that can be used to change the meaning of a word in a language, e.g. the /s/ and /z/ sounds in *hiss* and *his*.

phonetics   The area of linguistics which deals with the production, classification and perception of speech sounds.

phonology   In linguistics, the study of the system of sounds in a particular language or between languages, their distribution and patterning, and the contrastive relationships between the sounds.

pidgin   Pidgins are a reduced, simplified means of communication, often a mix of two languages, developed to facilitate basic communication where there is no common language. They are strongly associated with trade routes, trading posts and plantation colonies, and have historically often arisen from contact between European (e.g. French, English, Portuguese, Dutch) and non-European languages.

pragmatics   The study of language in use, and particularly how language works together with context in order to produce meaning.

realisation   Realisation occurs when an abstract unit of linguistic analysis is produced in actual language. So phonemes, for example, are realised in actual speech sounds.

Received Pronunciation (RP)   The accent traditionally associated with educated British speakers, predominantly in the southeast of England, which is sometimes presented (e.g. in teaching of English as a Foreign Language) as 'standard' British English pronunciation. It is actually used by only a small proportion of UK speakers, and while it is often referred to as a 'prestige' accent, it can also be viewed negatively in some social contexts, especially in its more marked form.

register   Register refers to the way a speaker or writer uses language differently in different contexts. The register is hence the sum of the communicative choices and adjustments you make when communicating with others according to the social situation, the relationship between the participants and the reason for the interaction (e.g. degree of formality/informality, hedging and mitigation, politeness/impoliteness).

repertoire   Repertoire or linguistic repertoire is the name given to the totality of the languages, varieties, dialects, styles, registers, accents and so on that an individual has at their command.

semantics   In linguistics, the branch of the subject which deals with the study of meaning.

sentence   A sentence is a written grammatical unit consisting of at least one *independent clause* – i.e. as a minimum, a subject and a verb. However, a sentence usually also consists of other parts of speech (object, adjective, preposition etc.) and often of more than one clause as in: Although it's the weekend (1), she can't come to the party (2), because she's working (3). In this example 1 and 3 are each dependent clauses and 2 is independent. See *clause* above.

slang   Slang is non-standard and informal language that expresses something in a new way. It might be associated with a particular group or generation of speakers, and is usually transient and rapidly-changing – though some slang expressions survive for a long time, and some make their way into what is considered mainstream language.

sociolect   A characteristic variety of a language shared by a particular set of speakers, often defined by social grouping or social class.

Standard English   Standard English is the name given to a substantially regularised variety of English which over time has come to be regarded as broadly acceptable and understood wherever English is used. It is the form most often associated with educated or formal speaking or writing – though it can be spoken in any accent, and the spoken and written forms are not always identical.

standard language   A standard language is the variety of a language that is generally considered the dominant and most prestigious form of that language. It has usually been codified over time, and is the form most often encountered in 'standard' dictionaries and grammars of the language. It might have some special legal status within a country, and might even be considered or claimed by some to be simply the 'correct' form of the language.

text   In linguistics, a text is more than simply a piece of writing. A text is an instance of meaningful communication – whether spoken, written, gestured, drawn or a combination of any or all of these communicative modes.

tonal language   A tonal language is one in which words can differ in spoken tone (or pitch) as well as in vowels and consonants in order to distinguish meaning. Hence in Thai (which has five tones), for example, *mai* spoken with a falling tone means 'not', while *mai* with low tone means 'new'.

translanguaging   An analytical approach to the language behaviour of bilingual or multilingual speakers which foregrounds the idea of their various languages forming a single, integrated competence rather than two or more separate, discrete competences.

utterance A unit or section of spoken language (which may be as short as a single word, for example an exclamation like *Help!*), identifiable as a unit because it is separated by pauses or silence. Linguists avoid using the word 'sentence' when talking about speech, as the sentence is a unit of *written* text.

well-formed/ill-formed An utterance is said to be well-formed if it conforms to the grammatical rules of a language or dialect, whether standard or non-standard, and ill-formed if it does not.

Index

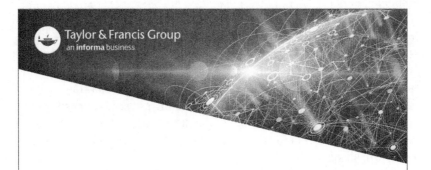